DOCUMENTS AND PLANS

SUBMITTED BY THE

WATER COMMITTEE,

TO THE

COMMON COUNCIL

OF THE

CITY OF BROOKLYN,

FOR THE YEAR 1854.

ORDERED PRINTED.

BROOKLYN:
JOHN W. HEIGHWAY, & Co., PRINTERS,
MORNING JOURNAL NEWSPAPER OFFICE,
21 COURT STREET.
1854.

CONTENTS:

―――o―――

PAGE.

DOCUMENT No. ONE:

Report of the Water Committee of the City of Brooklyn, made to the Common Council, March 13th. 1854; With the Report of Gen. Ward B. Burnett, Civil Engineer, on the Introduction of a Supply of Water, ... 5

DOCUMENT No. TWO:

Specifications Accompanying the Report of March 13th. 1854, ... 41

DOCUMENT No. THREE:

Estimates of Cost in Detail, ... 57

DOCUMENT No. FOUR:

Report of Samuel McElroy, Principal Assistant Engineer, on the Final Location of the Conduit and Canal, 65

DOCUMENT No. FIVE:

List of Maps and Plans, ... 71

DOCUMENT No. SIX:

Proposition of H. S. Welles & Co., for the Construction of the Works, ... 73

DOCUMENT No. SEVEN:

Correspondence with the Long Island Water Works Company, and H. S, Welles & Co., . . . 75

DOCUMENT No. EIGHT:

Outline of Plan for Supplying the City of Brooklyn with Water, submitted to the Electors June 1, 1854, 85

DOCUMENT No. NINE:

Report of John S. Stoddard, City Surveyor, on the Subject of Supplying Brooklyn with Water, by the Well System, ... 87

DOCUMENT No. TEN:

Report of Water Committee September 18th, 1854, submitting the Report of Robert Leigh, George Stoddard, and J. Carson Brevoort Esquires, on the Gaugings of the Long Island Ponds. . . 101

DOCUMENT No. ELEVEN:

Brooklyn Water Law, passed June 3d. 1852, with Amendments passed, ... 107

DOCUMENT No. TWELVE:

Outline of Plan, submitted to the Electors, July 11th 1853. 117

DOCUMENT No. THIRTEEN:

Report of Progress on the Water Question, submitted by the Water Committee to the Common Council of the City of Brooklyn, December, 1854. 119

PLATES.

FRONTISPIECE	Plan of Pumping Engine.
PLATE No. 1.	General Map.
" 2.	Conduit Line, Sheet No. 1.
" 3.	" 2.
" 4.	Canal " 3.
" 5.	" " 4.
" 6.	" " 5.
" 7.	Distributing Reservoir.
" 8.	Receiving "
" 9.	Supply No. 1.
" 10.	" 2.
" 11.	" 3.
" 12.	" 4.
" 13.	Keeper's House—Distributing Reservoir.
" 14.	Gate " " "
" 15.	" " " (Plan.)
" 16.	Carriage Entrance "
" 17.	Engine House Elevation.
" 18.	" " Plan and Section.
" 19.	Dam and Apron.
" 20.	Road Bridge.
" 21.	Farm "
" 22.	Creek Culverts.
" 23.	Box "
" 24.	Waste Weir " Conduit.
" 25.	" " Canal.
" 26.	Sections, Conduit and Canal.
" 27.	Gate and Keeper's House.

DOCUMENT, NO. ONE.

REPORT

OF THE

WATER COMMITTEE,

OF THE

CITY OF BROOKLYN,

MADE TO THE

COMMON COUNCIL

MARCH 13TH, 1854;

WITH THE REPORT OF

GEN. WARD B. BURNETT,

CIVIL ENGINEER;

ON THE INTRODUCTION OF A

SUPPLY OF WATER.

REPORT

OF THE

WATER COMMITTEE.

The Committee on Water, to whom was referred so much of the annual Message of His Honor, the Mayor, as relates to Water, for an early report, do report accordingly:

They present herewith a Plan to supply the city with water for the determination of the Common Council, and with its authority, for the approval of the electors in pursuance of the provisions of the Act of the Legislature, passed June 3d, 1853.

The Committee would imperfectly discharge their duty if they did not explain fully the views which have governed their action, and the reasons for the adoption of the proposed plan. They will, therefore, do so in as succinct a manner as the importance of the subject will permit.

A consideration of a peculiar character pressed itself forward at the onset. The plan submitted to the people in July last, and which failed to meet their sanction, was the only feasible one, as regards the sources of supply, within the power of Brooklyn. Five or six years of agitation of the question, and of public discussion, and of professional examination of the most experienced engineers, had settled that no dependence could be placed for an adequate supply for the future upon wells, or the Croton, or the ponds on Long Island, each of which modes has had, in turn, its advocates. The streams alone which, with a steady volume and almost unmatched purity, having their origin in the hilly portions of Long Island, and increasing in bulk from the springs which line their course, find their way to the great bays on the south side, were the only sources upon which dependence could be placed, and that plan accordingly proposed to derive water from them.

The expense for a daily supply of five millions of gallons, adding a capital to represent the expense of raising the water, was estimated according to the prices of labor and materials in 1852, at three millions, seven hundred and sixty thousand dollars, and for a daily supply of thirty millions of gallons for the works alone at $7,467,295, and adding a capital to represent the expense of running the engines at $10,419,998.

Many influences concurred to defeat the plan thus proposed, but the most material objections, and those which took most firmly hold of the public mind were, first, the uncertainty of the quantity of water to be derived from the streams, especially as a portion of them had been secured to the Long Island Water Works Company; and secondly, the enormous expense of the works as estimated, and the liability of increased expense beyond the estimates according to all experience when expensive improvements of a public character have been performed by public agents.

In considering this popular decision, the Committee were forced to regard it as determining the unwillingness of our citizens to put at hazard without further investigation and better satisfaction, even a determinate, much less an unlimited amount of money for the purpose. They believed, however, that all classes of the community were desirous of having a supply of water introduced into the city, adequate to all the objects of domestic, sanitary, protective, and manufacturing purposes; commensurate with the wants, conveniences and ease of the people, and on a plan as comprehensive as the prospects for future population, wealth and municipal character of our city required.

They have, therefore, been compelled in obedience to the public sentiment, to review the whole subject, and in doing so they have been aided both by the professional skill and experience of the distinguished engineer employed by them, under the authority of the Board, as well as of the prior labors of Mr McAlpine, and by the advice and encouragement of those gentlemen who have preceded them in this duty, and especially of Charles R. Marvin, Esq., who has put at their disposal all the memoranda and documents which were made and collected by him during his arduous labors as Chairman of the Water Committee of the last Board. Without this assistance, it is hardly necessary to say, that the Committee could not have attempted thus early to comply with the resolution referred to them.

The Committee are satisfied that we must look to the streams before alluded to for water for Brooklyn. The examinations of the engineers, and the gauging observations made through the summer and fall of 1852, have demonstrated that they will afford an ample supply for a century to come, if the population of the city should continue to increase as it has already done, by extending the works so as to embrace the streams beyond those now contemplated to be taken. Assuming fifty gallons a day for each inhabitant, which is the quantity supplied in New York, seven millions of gallons will be wanted for present use, taking our population to be one hundred and forty thousand. This allowance includes a liberal margin for protection from fire and for manufacturing purposes, and with twenty millions of gallons per day, the quantity yielded by the streams now to be taken, will supply a population of four hundred thousand souls, and provide for all the requirements of manufactures and extinguishment of fires.

The supply upon the plan which the Committee have determined to propose, will be greatly increased beyond that under the former one. According to Mr McAlpine's report, the quantity of water which may be obtained in the driest seasons of the year, from the following streams is estimated to be,

		Gals. per day.
Jamaica Creek,		5,000,000
Springfield Creek,	West Branch,	1,500,000
" "	East "	250,000
Hook "	West "	4,000,000
	Galls.	10,750,000

							Amount brought forward			10,750,000
"	"	Middle	"	.	.	.	.	.	.	500,000
"	"	East	"	.	.	.	.	.	.	2,000,000
Pines	"			.	.	.	.	.	.	2,000,000
Parsonage	"			.	.	.	.	.	.	10,000,000
		Total,		.	.	.	.	.	.	25,250,000

Of these, Jamaica Creek, Springfield Creek, West Branch, Hook Creek and Parsonage Creek, discharging together a minimum quantity of over twenty millions of gallons, had been secured by the L. I. Water Works Company, prior to the act of June 3, 1853, which protects the property of that Company in them. If the rights of that Company be extinguished, this quantity may be added to that contemplated in the former plan; inasmuch as it was excluded from it, though included in Mr McAlpine's report, which was made prior to the purchases of that Company, and before the passage of the act just mentioned. It appears, however, that a fact of the greatest importance was not taken into consideration. The dams constructed at the different streams, for the purpose of making the necessary head, in order to enable the water to run with a proper current through the conduit, would throw the water back, and more or less according to the height of the dams, repress the springs which materially contribute to the volume of the streams. The lower down the streams the discharge can be kept, the greater the quantity of water; while the higher the level of the discharge the less the quantity, in consequence of stopping the springs, which have a lower source themselves. In examining the record of gauging kept by Mr Whitlock in 1852 under the direction of the Water Committee, for that year, we find the following entry for the week ending Dec. 14, 1852. "During the past week I have drawn P. Cornell's pond to a low head, then shut the gates. It rose steadily until within three inches of a full head. It then increased less and less until at the final gauging it showed but one-half the quantity of water of the former trial. Trial No. 1. with a low head in pond, shows 6,597,000 gallons per day, while Trial No. 1, with a full head in pond, only shows 3,109,214 gallons per day. The important fact of repression of the springs is thus experimentally established. The loss of water from this circumstance, throughout the whole route, would be so great as materially to affect the estimate of water above given, if the close conduit were adopted, which requires a descent of from four to six inches to the mile. In order to obviate this difficulty, a change of plan will be necessary. It is therefore proposed to bring the water in an open canal to Baisley's pond, connecting it with the different ponds and streams, and thence by conduit to the well, from which it will be pumped into the reservoir.

The descent, to be provided for the flow of water in the canal, is only two inches in the mile.

In order the further to provide against the possibility of a failure, it is proposed to make that portion of the works which may now be constructed of sufficient capacity to admit of an extension for a daily supply of forty millions of gallons and to meet extraordinary cases of drought or accident to the distributing reservoir, which will be located on Cypress Hills, will be so constructed as by means of three compartments or distinct chambers, to hold a reserve quantity of about two hundred millions of gallons, and capable of furnishing sufficient water for twenty-eight days for the present population of the city. With such modifications of the former plan, the Commmittee think there can be no reasonable doubt of an adequate supply.

The next enquiry was as to the cost of the works. By the change of the site of the reservoir from Prospect Hill, where an excavation was to have been made to contain the water for distribution, and placing it on Cypress Hills, where nature has herself formed one of treble the dimensions, a large expense will be saved and a head of water at a height of 172 feet obtained for the distributing pipes capable of being carried by its own hydrostatic pressure to the height of fifty feet above the level of the corner of Henry and Pierrepont streets.

The latter site has been purchased for the Long Island Water Works Company now held by them.

A further material reduction of the expense will be effected by the adoption of Ball's patent indestructable water pipe in place of the common iron one. The oxidation of the iron pipe and the formation of turbercles on the inner surface, where the water is very pure, have of late attracted the serious attention of practical men as well as the learned. While the former process is more gradual, it being estimated that from three-tenths to four-tenths of an inch in depth of cast iron one inch thick will be destroyed in a century in clear water, the formation of nodules or tubercles is so rapid as to produce an alarming diminution of the capacity of iron pipes in a few years.

The City Engineer of Boston in his report to the Cochituate Water Board in 1852, says " all the large pipes that have been opened have been partially or entirely covered on the inner surfaces, some with detached tubercles varying from a half to two and a half inches base, with a depth or thickness in the middle of from one quarter to three quarters of an inch. The Jamaica acqueduct pipe which was originally ten inches in diameter has been in some cases, reduced to eight by tubercles." The same effect has been observed in France.

The patented water pipe remains free from corrosion and incrustation. It is formed of iron, coated internally and externally with hydraulic cement, and is said to be preferable, for other reasons as well as those stated, to the best iron pipes.

Our fellow citizen Joseph A. Perry, Esq., informs the Committee that it is so preferable, and that water is forced through it at the Greenwood Cemetery grounds where it is in use, to an elevation of over one hundred feet.

In the discharge of their duties the Committee have obtained the assistance of Gen. Ward B. Burnett, U. S. Engineer, who has, under their direction, prepared the plans herewith submitted, the specifications of the work and estimate of the expense, which will explain in detail the mode proposed to be adopted.

This plan, as before observed, contemplates the construction of works adequate to the supply of twenty millions of gallons of water daily, with a capacity for an increase to forty millions of gallons. Two engines only will be erected at present, capable of pumping ten millions of gallons each daily. Eighty miles of pipe will be laid for the present wants of the city, and eight hundred hydrants provided. The whole expense of these works, including engines and pipes, according to General Burnett's estimates, will be $4,025,000—add for land and interest and expenses as hereinafter mentioned $475,000, making in all $4,500,000.

If water can be supplied in this quantity and at this cost, the people of Brooklyn will be satisfied. A comparison of the means and resources of this city, as compared with the ability of New York under similiar circumstances, will satisfy every candid mind of the propriety of the expenditure.

New York commenced the Croton works in 1835, when her population was 270,000, and her taxable property, $217,000,000, at a cost of $13,000,000. The liability which the citizens of New York assumed was therefore, at the time, more than $48 for each inhabitant, and over six per cent. of the taxable property.

The taxable property of Brooklyn by the books of the assessors of last year, amounts to about $67,000,000.

The population, before estimated, is 140,000.

At an expense of four millions and a half of dollars, the whole cost will not amount to thirty-three dollars for each inhabitant, and will be less than seven per cent. of the taxable property, if the debt were to be paid off at once, and the water made entirely free.

No one will doubt that the introduction of such a supply of water will enhance the value of the real estate of the city more than that amount the instant the plan shall be adopted.

The payment of the principal debt, will, however be postponed, and it will be necessary to provide for the interest only.

This will amount to $270,000 annually: to which it will be necessary to add $30,000 for expenses of running the works, making an annual charge of $300,000, equal to a taxation of forty-six cents on the hundred dollars, or a Poll tax of two dollars and fifteen cents for each inhabitant. This is based on the idea of free water. If, on the other hand, the same rates be charged for the water as are charged in New York, the income from the works will be, on the basis of the receipts in New York for 1850, which is the last year that a census was taken, and after deducting all expenses except those of running the engines, $124,000, immediately, with our present population.

But in any calculation of this kind there are other considerations which must be regarded. The rates of insurance will be materially reduced; the difference between those charged on property here and those on property in New York, being thirty per cent. in favor of the latter. This difference will disappear as soon as a supply of water is introduced: Besides this, the additional attraction to Brooklyn as a place of residence, in consequence of such supply will add numbers to our population, and wealth to our tax roll, beyond what would otherwise be added. In a few years we will present the most favorable comparison with our sister city. Perhaps, in less time than has elapsed since the commencement of her water works, we will exhibit a population equal in numbers to hers at present with only one third of her present water debt. It is impossible to appreciate exactly the amount of benefit from these two sources. Assuming the amount paid for premiums of Insurance on Brooklyn property as estimated by intelligent underwriters to amount annually to $250,000, the yearly amount saved to insurers by the reduction of premiums immediately will be $75,000.

It is more difficult to give even an approximate statement in dollars and cents of the advantage from the increase in population, and the committee will not attempt it.

They believe there can be no difference of opinion as to the propriety of the expenditure for obtaining the results proposed. The question remains, can these results be accomplished?

In order to put at rest all cavil or objection in regard to the cost, the Committee deem it advisable to put the construction of the entire work under contract, provided it can be done within the estimate of the Engineer. By such a course, not only will the expense of the water department of the city be materially diminished from what it would otherwise be with its large corps of officials, but the danger of excess of expenditure beyond estimates arising from the temptation to prolong the work, and the irresponsibility of public agents will be altogether avoided. It will be the duty of the Water Commissioners to see that the work is faithfully done, while the Engineer employed by the city, with his assistants and inspectors of masonry and other work, will keep them constantly advised of the progress of the work and the manner of its execution. It is considered a wise economy in private affairs to contract out work, and there is no reason why it should not be done in public works. In fact, the act authorizing the construction of the works contemplates its being done by contracts for particular parts, but not as an entirety. The Committee therefore recommend the passage of a law by the Legislature to amend the act so as to permit a contract to be made by the Common Council for the whole work, and to limit the amount authorised to be raised for the expense to four millions and a half of dollars, exclusive of interest during the time of construction. This time will not exceed two years for the entire completion of the work, and the Committee are assured that the works can be so far completed in one year as to supply water at the end of that period, providing the engines can be built.

The estimated expense, therefore, of the entire work, is as follows:

For the construction of the works complete, with 80 miles of pipe, according to the estimate of the Engineer	$4,025,000
For the extinguishment of the title of the Long Island Water Works Company to the streams and reservoir site owned by them, and vesting the same in the City of Brooklyn	150,000
For amount already expended by the city for the streams and real estate purchased by it	44,600
For expenses of Water Commissioners, Engineers and Assistants, Clerks, Inspectors and Superintendents $23,000 a year for two years	46,000
For cost of land yet to be acquired, and for damages to owners of land by reason of the construction of the works	100,000
For interest on $4,500,000 for an average of one year $270,000, but if a supply be introduced in one year the average will be for six months.	135,000
Total	$4,500,000

Competent and responsible parties have proposed to build the works at the cost estimated by the Engineer and to purchase the property and privileges of the Long Island Water Works Company and vest the same in the city. They will also guarantee the supply of water on the plan proposed to equal the capacity of the two engines to be erected to pump up, namely: twenty millions of gallons daily; leaving ten per cent. of the contract price in the Treasury of the City until such guaranty shall be in all respects discharged, and the works completely finished according to the plans and specifications under the supervision of the Engineers to be appointed by the City, and subject to the final approval of the Water Commissioners.

The Committee forbear making any remarks upon the necessity for water. That era in the history of the City of Brooklyn is passed. The day of discussion on that point has gone by. The public mind is concluded upon it, and the question is not whether we ought to have water; but How shall we best obtain it? New York boldly undertook the Croton enterprise with more responsibility than we now propose to assume, and a rich reward has awaited her. That city is now conceded to be as desirable a place of residence as any one in the United States; and under the influence of the liberal policy which she has adopted in regard to water and its consequent sewerage, her settled limits have expanded in a ratio far beyond anything in her previous history. It is in no envious spirit that we thus refer to her, but rather as an example which Brooklyn has had so close by her side, as to familiarize the minds of our citizens to the necessity of procuring a bountiful supply of this indispensable element of nature.

With this necessity admitted, we have only to be satisfied that water can be obtained within the compass of our means to have the work accomplished.

The Committee have addressed themselves to this point, and feel confident that, if they have not presented the very best plan, they at least submitted an entirely feasible one, and one that should be adopted, should no better one be presented.

They refer to the accompanying report of Gen. Burnett, for the details of the work. They also append to the report an outline of the plan to be submitted to the people at an early day for their decision.

BROOKLYN, March 13, 1854.

JOHN A. DAYTON,
R. C. BRAINARD,
D. P. BARNARD,
F. G. QUEVEDO,
} Water Committee.

CIVIL ENGINEER'S REPLIES TO QUESTIONS PROPOSED BY THE WATER COMMITTEE.

BROOKLYN, *New York, March* 11, 1854.

JOHN A. DAYTON, ESQ.,
Chairman of the Brooklyn Water Committee.

SIR,
In compliance with your note of the 3d instant, I have nearly finished a report for the Committe you represent; but as you particularly desired an early reply to the questions therein propounded, I send it herewith, requesting that upon the receipt of the report, you will oblige me by appending it to the following answers:

Question No. 1.—"Is it customary to give contracts for the entire completion of a public work, including all the incidental expenses, except those immediately required for supervision and inspection on the part of the proprietors of the work, to insure its proper construction, in accordance with the plans and specifications furnished by them?"

Answer. This has been done in many cases:—The entire work on the "Ohio and Mississippi" Railroad, involving an amount of $9,000,000; the "Albany and Susquehannah," "Rome and Watertown," "Chicago, Rock Island and Council Bluffs," "Toledo and St. Louis," "Fort Wayne and Chicago," "Louisville and Nashville," "Williamsport and Elmira," "Catawissa and Muncey," "Tamagua and Catawissa," "Cleveland and Columbus," Lackawana and Bloomsburgh Railroads; the Buffalo Water Works, and many other public works in the United States, are either built or under contract in this way. There is no difference of principle involved between a single contract for a work, or a subdivision of contracts for the same work, and it has this advantage to the proprietors where the work is let for a specific sum, and guaranteed as to its results; that the additions of cost to the original estimates by extra work and otherwise, which occur in most public works, are avoided.

The cost of the Croton Aqueduct to the City of New York, is nearly four times the estimate for its construction as sanctioned by a vote of the people; the cost of the Albany Water Works has been twice the amount appropriated in the charter, and as a general rule, it is much more safe and economical to let such a work as this under carefully prepared plans and specifications and proper supervision, than to do it under specified prices for materials and labor.

Question No. 2. State what work is necessary to be done, and estimate, as near as you can, the number of assistants that should be employed by the Corporation for its performance, upon the supposition that the line of Water Works is to be completed and in operation in two years.

B

Answer. The proposed modifications of the plans and line are completed, though not entirely ready for publication. The specifications I enclose herewith. The cost of this preliminary work, exclusive of my own services, will be about $900.

The *centre line* of the conduit and the *precise* position of all the structures, should be *deffinitely* located by your own engineers. It will be desirable to have for these services, and afterward for the superintendence and supervision of the work in the course of its construction; one chief engineer, one principal assistant, one chief draughtsman, one chief clerk, one assistant clerk and draughtsman, and one messenger attatched to the offices at the City Hall, Brooklyn. One resident engineer, one draughtsman to trace the *working plans*, and to use the compass when required, one rodman, and a chainman stationed near the engine house, and another party of the same strength at Baiseley's. In addition to these, it will be well to employ, from time to time, when required, one superintendent of machinery at the work shops, a number of inspectors of masonry, superintendents for laying pipes, and 1 superintendent of carpentry, to be stationed at those points on the line where they may be required, further to insure the proper construction of the work.

Question No. 3.—Is it your opinion that it is the policy of the city to pay for the entire completion of the works, the sum of $4,025,000?

Answer.—I have estimated the work to be done on a plan essentially the same as the one proposed, more than one year ago; and since then I have carefully revised that estimate; and now again, at your request, have gone over the whole work with reference to the modifications to which you have called my attention; and I am firmly of the opinion, that contractors cannot realize more than a reasonable profit upon the construction of the work for the sum of $4,025,000.

Question No. 4.—Will a contract, based upon the estimate of $4,025,000, be sufficiently remunerative to insure the completion of the work?

Answer.—I think that it will be remunerative. But if it should not be, the corporation may be secured against loss by the *large* per centage retained from estimates; and by the established credit and character of the gentlemen who may be employed to construct, and to guarantee the construction of the work.

Question No. 5.—Is the aggregate supply of water flowing from Baiseley's, Nostrand's, Simonson's, P. Cornwell's, and L. Cornwell's Ponds, equal to a supply of 20,000,000 gallons daily, and can that amount be doubled when required by proceeding eastward, and can that increased quantity be delivered at the engine-house by the line of work as projected?

Answer.—The quantity of water flowing from the six ponds named in your question, has been ascertained by a careful series of gaugings, made by my directions in the fall of 1852, which was a very dry season; and the results then obtained, were verified by the gaugings made for the corporation of Brooklyn during that year. I append to this answer the amount of water flowing from each pond at that time, and the aggregate; under the firm conviction that the clearing out and extension of some of the beds of those ponds will give us an increased supply, and render certain and constant, the aggregate amount required.

As far as relates to doubling the supply of 20,000,000 gallons daily, I have only to remark that the work will be constructed according to the plans for passing 40,000,000 of gallons daily to the engine-house, and that if that very large supply cannot be furnished during seasons of great drought, by introducing the discharge of all the ponds as far as the Massapequa, we have only to go eastward a few miles further, to obtain at a small additional expense, all that may be required from the continuation of the same series of ponds; which are almost as numerous as the many indentations of the coast of Long Island, and seldom more than three miles apart.

	Daily discharge.
Baisley's Pond, Jamaica Creek,	5,400,000 gallons.
Nostrand's Pond,	1,700,000 "
Simonson's Pond, West Branch Hook Creek,	3,600,000 "
P. Cornwell's Pond, East do. do.	3,000,000 "
L. Cornwell's Pond, Parsonage Creek,	9,300,000 "
Aggregate daily supply fron the five ponds named,	23,000,000 "
To which may be added at a future day,	
Springfield Creek,	400,000 "
Pine's Pond, Pine's Creek,	2,200,000 "
Willis's Pond, East Meadow Creek,	7,000,000 "
Jones's Pond,	3,200,000 "
Massapequa Pond,	5,100,000 "
	17,900,000 "
Aggregate daily supply from all the Ponds as far as Massapequa,	40,900,000 "

Question, No. 6.—Have you any evidence of the purity of the water, and do you believe that the canal connections between the ponds, will render the water, when delivered at the distributing reservoirs, less pure than it is in the ponds at present?

I append herewith the analysis made by Dr James R. Chilton, an analytical chemist, well known in your community, as the best answer that can be given in regard to the purity of the water; only observing that we have no record of any water having been introduced in any city in the world, more pure than these waters of Long Island, with the exception of Boston, in favor of which there is an unimportant difference.

	Grains of impurities per gallon in decimals.
Baiseley's Pond, Jamaica Creek,	2.720
Simonson's Pond, West Branch Hook Creek,	2.000
L. Cornwell's Pond, Parsonage Creek,	2.800
Willis's Pond, East Meadow Creek,	2.000
Massapequa,	2.880

In reply to that portion of the question, asking whether the open canal connections between the ponds, will affect the purity of the water at the distributing reservoir, at Cypress

Hill, I have to say; that it is my belief that the use of the open canal will not lessen the purity of the waters, for the following reasons. Some of these ponds are supplied by springs, brooks, and streams, which pass through the towns of Hempstead, Jamaica, and other densely settled places, and still discharge waters of unquestioned purity. Besides, the waters of all the ponds will be collected in the enlarged pond at Baiseley's, as a receiving reservoir in a state of quiescence, where any impurity held in suspension, which may have been acquired in their course thither, may be deposited.

The *closed* conduit leaves the receiving reservoir upon the other side of the pond. Through this conduit the water, after having been settled and filtered, will flow in all its purity to the engine-house, and thence by the rising main to the distributing reservoir, at Cypress Hill.

Question No. 7.—Will it be necessary under your plan of the works, to raise the surface of any of the ponds as above named, in connection with the projected line?

Answer.—It is possible that it may be necessary to raise the levels of Baiseley's and L. Cornwell's ponds a few inches. The test level we are now running will determine that point. We can reduce the level of the surfaces of the ponds between Baiseley's and Leonard Cornwell's and thus, I believe, insure a greater discharge from each of them.

Question No. 8.—Do you think it objectionable to raise the surface of the ponds, and if so, for what reason?

Answer.—I do, and for reasons which appear more fully in my report, which I shall only briefly illustrate in this answer.

We obtained permission to lower the surface of Douglass's pond at the head of Little Neck Bay, in the summer of 1852; and the experiment, carefully performed, resulted in an increased discharge of water after every reduction of the head, and an increased discharge of about one third, when the pond was lowered only two feet six inches. I am informed by your honorable committee that similar results followed similar experiments under Mr Whitlock, the engineer employed to gauge the water for the city of Brooklyn.

I obtained the sections of more than 100 wells, generally from those who dug them, as well to inform myself of the stratification, as to learn something of the height of the great source of water under Long Island, known as "*the main spring.*"

I found it under and near the centre of the Island, to stand at about 25 feet above high tide; and at a less height as we approached the sea coast, where the springs frequently break out below high water mark. I have also observed, that the most copious springs that flow from the Island, are very seldom more than ten feet above high tide. An impervious dam, as high as their sources, say ten feet, would therfore suppress them; and force them to seek a lower outlet, in the strata of sand and gravel of the surrounding country. The same remark may be made of those springs which have higher sources, and, I think, the experiments made at Douglass' and other ponds so conclusive, that I recommend you by all means to avoid raising the surfaces of the ponds to any extent; as, I believe, that every foot of rise in the surface of a pond in almost any locality, would suppress some of the sources which supply it with water.

Question No. 9.—Do you think that the sum of $475,000, will be sufficient to cover the cost of purchasing the title to lands for the line of conduit, for the structures, &c., and for the expenses of engineering, superintendence and contingencies?

Answer.—After a careful estimate of the value of the lands required and the damages that may be incurred, &c., I think that under a proper and judicious management, the sum of $475,000 will cover all such expenses; as well as those that must be incurred for engineering, superintendence, and the contingencies of that department.

I have the honor to be,

Very respectfully yours,

WARD B. BURNETT,

Civil Engineer.

REPORT

MADE TO THE

WATER COMMITTEE,

OF

THE COMMON COUNCIL

OF THE

CITY OF BROOKLYN,

MARCH, 1854,

ON A

PROPOSED PLAN FOR THE INTRODUCTION OF WATER,

BY

GEN'L. WARD B. BURNETT.

CIVIL ENGINEER.

BROOKLYN, *March*, 1854.

To

Messrs. JOHN A. DAYTON, R. C. BRAINARD, D. P. BARNARD, F. G. QUEVEDO, *and* SAMUEL BOOTH, ESQUIRES, *Water Committee of the Common Council of the City of Brooklyn;*

GENTLEMEN,

I have the honor to submit to your consideration a Report of Examinations, made at your request, for the introduction and distribution in this city, of a daily supply of Twenty Millions of gallons of water, from sources on Long Island, with a prospective increase to a daily supply of Forty Millions of gallons, together with Plans, Specifications, and Estimates for the same.

WARD B. BURNETT,
Civil Engineer.

REPORT.

The large population which has for a few years past rapidly accumulated in the City of Brooklyn and its vicinity, has had no other supply of water for either domestic or general use, than such as could be furnished from the cisterns, and wells constructed by individual effort, or corporate authority; the supply thus obtained being entirely inadequate to their present, and much less to their prospective wants.

The importance of furnishing every large community with an abundance of pure and wholesome water, as well for its beneficial effects on the health and comfort of the residents, as for its safeguard to property, scarcely needs argument. In the case under consideration, the absence of such a supply has made practical demonstration of the consequent evils, not only in the insecurity of property from fire and the high rates of insurance; but in the unwholesome character of the water generally used, and its effects on the health and comfort of the citizens.

The interest which the subject of water supplies has accquired throughout the country, as well as in those districts most in need of this relief, has made it an object of general attention; and to the engineer it presents a wide range of experimental research, involving some of the most interesting laws of nature.

The attention of the corporate authority of Brooklyn has been directed to this question for a number of years past. In December, 1847, Messrs D. A. Bokee, John Stanbury, and J. W. Cochran, special committee on this subject, submitted a report, containing a letter from the late Major D. B. Douglass, one of the most eminent engineers of this country, favorable to an adequate supply of water from the island.

In January, 1849, Messrs. George B. Fisk, Arthur W. Benson, George Hall. William McDonald, and J. W. Cochran, special committee on this subject, submitted a report of progress on the following points:—

"*First.*—As to a supply of water within the city limits, from wells and springs.

"*Second.*—As to a supply from the streams and ponds of the island.

"*Third.*—As to the quality of the water in each case.

"*Fourth.*—As to the cost of placing the water in a reservoir, as well as the cost of such a reservoir.

"*Fifth.*—The cost for fire purposes only; and the cost of pipes, &c., for all the uses of the city."

The report refers to examinations and experiments made by the Committee, and contains analyses of the water, together with an estimate of cost of $830,000, including "a reservoir on Prospect Hill, to contain eleven millions of gallons, and thirty-six miles of distribution pipe," &c. In the copy of the report in my possession, the amount of daily supply contemplated by the Committee is not given.

In December, 1851, Messrs. Charles R. Marvin, J. H. Smith, Edward Pell, Henry A. Kent, and E. B. Litchfield, standing committee on this subject, submitted a report, with communications from John B. Jervis and Wm. J. McAlpine, Esqs., civil engineers of eminence, on the feasibility and adequacy of a supply from the island sources.

In their report, the following allusion is made to the former action in this matter:—

"The Water Committee to whom was referred the annexed resolution, beg leave respectfully to report:—That in the discharge of their duty they have given a full consideration to the various plans heretofore proposed for supplying the city with water. The subject has not now for the first time engaged the attention of the Common Council. It has for years, been evident, that for protection against fire, the interests of our citizens required a more adequate supply of water, than it was possible to obtain from the wells and cisterns in ordinary use. It has more recently become apparent that as our city increases, the water furnished from these wells will deteriorate; and it has therefore been considered as of great importance to devise a system which will afford not only a more abundant supply for the purpose of preventing the ravages of fire, but also of furnishing our citizens with pure and wholesome water for domestic uses.

"In 1847, the special committee having the subject in charge, made a report, which was published; and a farther report was made by a similar committee in 1849. In the views then expressed, and in the action of the Common Council upon other occasions, the importance of the subject in reference to the future growth and prosperity of our city was evidently perceived; and the Committee being themselves full impressed with the necessity which will be forced upon us at no very distant day, of definite action, have made such investigations as seemed to be required, in order to present to the Common Council a plan, feasible, and sufficient, not only for our immediate wants, but capable of extension, as our increasing population might render necessary."

In April, 1852, the same Committee submitted a report in detail from William J. McAlpine Esq., civil engineer, with estimates and plans, based on several amounts of supply from the streams entering Jamaica and Hempstead bays, on the south side of Long Island.

The report is worthy of attention, as the first professional examination made from surveys of the contemplated sources by the City of Brooklyn, and it contains much valuable information.

My attention has for a long period been directed to this subject, as well for the rapidly increasing demands of the populous vicinity of Brooklyn, (soon to be consolidated with it,) as for the city proper; and I have had occasion to examine carefully the several projects of supply from artificial wells of large diameter, from the ponds on the northern shore of the island and also from those of the southern shore.

The results of these examinations are embodied in the plan herewith presented for your consideration; and the preference is given to the series of streams near the southern shore of Long Island, for many very important reasons.

The purposes to which a proper supply of water is available in a city are for

>Domestic Use,
>Manufactures,
>Extinction of Fires.
>Public Baths,
>Public Fountains,
>Street Cleansing, and
>Sewerage.

These are all important to the sanitary regulations of every community, though not all absolutely necessary. Individual efforts may provide to a limited extent for some of these uses; but the supply can never be otherwise than limited, and will but partially meet the requirements of a large population.

The various sources of supply available in a general or limited form, for a city, may be derived from

>Rain Water, or Surface Drainage,
>Wells,
>Rivers and Lakes.
>Springs and Brooks.

In point of purity, so far as chemical tests are used, the rain water has the preference; although, beside atmospheric air, carbonic acid, and small portions of ammoniacal salts, are found in the purest varieties; perfectly pure water being obtained only by distillation.

In many cities of the Union, before the introduction of an adequate supply, under the controlling action of a fixed head, large cisterns were provided to collect the surface drainage of the streets, for use in case of fire, arranged with overflow pipes, by which the surplus received into the upper cistern was discharged into those below it. Cisterns also were provided to each house, the water in many cases being filtered for drinking and cooking purposes by permanent filters, through which the water thus needed was pumped.

It is found, however, in practice, that the impurities with which rain water becomes impregnated in its descent through the atmosphere of a city (especially in the vicinity of factories), and those which are carried from the roofs of the buildings into the cisterns, rapidly accumulate, and render the filter inoperative; and that frequent cleansing of the whole cistern is necessary on this account.

It is evident that the fiilters generally used for these cisterns are only of service in arresting the *mechanical* impurities of the water, and must soon be charged with a deposit, which chokes up the porous openings; while any chemical arrangement would as evidently need constant renewal. It is also evident that the quantity of the supply must depend on the *storing* capacity of the cistern, and the abundance or scarcity of rain; the quiescent state of the water depriving it to some extent of its proper supply of oxygen, and in other respects affecting its use.

While, therefore, a limited supply may be realized from rain water thus collected, the system is liable to many objections, and inadequate to other uses than those above named.

A second source of supply is found, generally by individual effort, in wells sunk to the flow-line of the various strata saturated with water, which fill them to a height proportional to the heads from which the subterranean sources are supplied.

In villages and districts sparsely settled, this is the most common method of supply, but where a compact population is found, and the wells derive their supply from the water percolating through the upper strata, they are impure and unwholesome; containing in some cities from 60 to 125 grains of impurities per gallon. This objection exists to some extent against many of the wells used in Brooklyn and vicinity, even where they are sunk so as to receive their supply from "*the Main Spring*" of the island, the water from which, beyond the limits of these places, is remarkably pure in quality and abundant in quantity. The character of this main source of supply which pervades the whole bed of the island is thus briefly sketched by me in a Report of September, 1852, upon the surveys made of the sources of water on the north side of Long Island:

"I can safely say that I have never known springs to maintain such a constant supply of water as those of Long Island, near its shores.

"They are very numerous, and discharge themselves copiously at the heads of the bays and indentations of the coast, at a little above the level of tide-water near the shores of the island; and from that level to twenty-five feet above high tide at the central part of the island, near Hempstead Plains, and other sandy wastes of less extent.

"I have made diligent inquiry of those who are experienced in well-digging, in different parts of the island, and the information obtained has confirmed me in the belief that the highest level of the hidden sources of water on Long Island, generally known by its citizens as "*the Main Spring*," is under these extensive plains of sand and near the centre of the island.

"I have also observed that but little of the rain which falls upon these plains, flows from them in brooks or streams; and that little remains upon the surface to be carried away by evaporation. Nearly all that falls sinks gradually to the depths below, percolating through strata of sand and gravel, occasionally interrupted by beds of clay and hard pan (which the sections of wells in that vicinity show are not continuous), and running again on their surface in currents more or less retarded, to openings in those strata, where the streams discharge themselves again into the sand and gravel beneath; until "*the Main Spring*," which is always found in a stratum of sand, thus receives nearly all the water that falls upon the plains, about 100 feet above its level.

"The annual average depth of rain, snow (melted), and dew which falls in England and Wales, has been determined to be about thirty-six inches.

"It is computed by Dr Dalton and others, who have given much attention to the subject, that about two thirds of this amount escapes in rivers, streams, surface springs, and by evaporation, leaving about one third to find its way to the great source of fresh water, known to exist under the Island of Great Britain.

"The average depth of water which has been known to fall on Long Island is about thirty-eight inches, and the extent of its surface is about 1,800 square miles; one half of which may be said to consist of a very porous sandy soil, which absorbs about two thirds of the water that falls upon it. The remainder of the surface of Long Island has its brooks and streams; but it may be said with safety, that only a small portion of the island is of such formation, as to retain the rain and melted snow upon its surface, in ponds lakes, or running brooks; to loose itself directly in the air of the ocean.

"It is reasonable to assert that at least one half of the water which falls upon the whole island is absorbed by the soil.

"Thus we have 5,280 by 5,280 feet by 1,800 square miles=50,181,120,000 square feet of surface, into 1 1-2 feet, or 66,998,160,000 cubic feet of water, which filters through strata of sand and gravel, slowly but surely, towards "*the Main Spring*," undiminished by drainage or evaporation, until it reaches the numerous springs and indentations near the coast, which mark and distinguish the topography of Long Island."

The vast supply of pure water furnished by clusters of springs to the ponds of Long Island, which very frequently have no other source; and the fact that these ponds sometimes derive their water from one spring alone, were the interesting phenomena, that induced me to make these few remarks, explanatory of the causes which should give us confidence in the great source of water, or "*the Main Spring*" of Long Island.

"It has been proposed to construct Artesian Wells, but they would not, in my opinion, be successful; for the reason that the channels of communication from the high grounds on the main shore are cut off by the deep recesses of the surrounding bays; and also, that if this were not the case, the dip of the strata of the main shore so far as I have observed it, is not favorable to such a project."

While careful examinations have satisfied me that for domestic use and manufactures, and in some cases for the extinction of fires, a supply from wells might meet the wants of a small community, the system cannot be complete in its operation, and involves the loss of other benefits, of great consequence to a city.

The third source of supply which has been used for cities, and furnishes water in sufficient quantities for all purposes, is found in the Rivers or Lakes on or near which they may be located.

In this country, as well as those of Europe, this has been a favorite resort. Philadelphia, Pittsburgh, Cincinnati, Chicago, New Orleans, and many other cities of the United States, are using the rivers or lakes on which they are situated, under circumstances peculiarly advantageous as to economy, and purity of supply.

Rivers are great physical arteries provided by nature for the benefit of the land and the air, and of those who live on the one and breathe the other. The effects of the gentle and unceasing process of evaporation from large streams and lakes upon the surrounding atmosphere, the consequent formations of dew, rain and snow, and their prominent uses to the vegetable and animal kingdoms, are all daily yielding to man their priceless benefits, while he finds abundant occupation in the pursuits of navigation and commerce. As sources of supply, rivers are of great value. One of the most effective methods of cleansing water from the mechanical impurities it may contain, is that of *subsidence* or deposit, and in this respect every large stream is a natural self-depurating reservoir. Gently flowing along its appointed course, and depositing by slow and sure process the matter over which gravity exercises control, its continued motion presents it to the action of the atmosphere, while it is carried to the foot of every city along its banks, with a never failing offering of one of the most necessary elements of life.

It rarely happens that the character of the bed over which it flows affects the water to an injurious extent, as in limestone countries; where the action of the atmosphere does much to counteract the *hardness* produced by the lime, with which the stream may be more or less impregnated.

In the case of Brooklyn and vicinity, however, the supply from such a source is out of the question, on account of the saltness of the East and North rivers, under the ebb and flow of the tides, and its great distance from any fresh water river of sufficient capacity.

Having been satisfied that the population of the western side of Long Island must be supplied from other sources than these enumerated, the next system, or that of springs and brooks, invites attention, and furnishes a satisfactory result. Nature has made provision for the necessities of this case, in the arrangement of the island, by which large springs supplying ponds for milling and manufacturing purposes, are formed along the northern and southern shores, which derive their supply from "*the Main Spring*" heretofore mentioned, and are remarkably constant in their flow throughout the year; while the purity and quality of the water, filtered through strata of sand and gravel, and delivered to us from that great *subterranean reservoir*, is seldom, if ever, surpassed.

Between Brooklyn and Hempstead Harbor, on the north side of the island, there are thirteen of these ponds; and within a similar distance on the southern shore there are eighteen ponds, deriving their principal sources by subterranean communication.

In consequence, however, of the location of the northern line of ponds, communication between them, by any connected line to Brooklyn, cannot be readily made, for the reason that they are separated by bold spurs of the main ridge, which involves the construction of a line of conduit either very circuitous, or very expensive.

While the northern slope thus projects abruptly, in prominent points, on the shore line; on the southern side, the fall is generally a gentle slope to the coast, and the ponds are much better adapted as to location and relative height, for the purpose in view. Their aggregate supply as far East as the Massapequa Pond only, in the driest season, is not less than forty millions of gallons per day, as may be seen by the following statements of the guaging made of the quantities discharged in the latter part of September and the month of October, 1852, which may be relied upon, as not far from the minimum discharge of the several ponds named:—

	Daily Discharge.
Baiseley's pond, Jamaica creek	5.400.000 galls.
Springfield creek	400.000 "
Nostrand's pond	1.900.000 "
Simonson's pond, West Branch Hook creek	3.600.000 "
P. Cornwell's pond, East do.	3.000.000 "
L. Cornwell's pond, Parsonage creek	9.300.000 "
Pine's pond, Pine creek	2.200.000 "
Willis' pond, East Meadow creek	7.000.000 "
Jones' pond	3.000.000 "
Massapequa pond	5.000.000 "
	40.800.000 galls.

The following analyses, stated in decimals, have been made of the waters of some of the principal streams by our distinguished chemist, Dr. James R. Chilton, showing the amount of impurities contained, viz:—

	Grains of impurities per gallon.
Jamaica Creek	2.720
West Branch of Hook Creek	2.000
Parsonage Creek	2.800
East Meadow Creek	2.000
Masapequa Pond	2.880

The following analyses of some of the waters of Brooklyn, from the several wells named, also by Dr. James R. Chilton, is here inserted, to show the great difference in the purity of these waters, and the water now used in this city:

	Grains of impurities per gallon.
Water from Well corner of Gold and Nassau streets, 5th Ward	38,400
" " " High and Jay " 2d "	58.640
" " " Fulton and Washington 4th "	46.440
" " Opposite Mansion House in Hicks " 3d "	43.200
" " Union street near Columbia, " 6th "	11.760
" " Corner of Douglass and Smith " 10th "	76.960

Having been requested by you to report on the introduction of twenty millions of gallons of water daily for present consumption, with a prospective increase to forty millions of gallons daily, I respectfully recommend the adoption of the system of supply embraced in the following:

DESCRIPTION OF THE PLAN.

This description will include the
DISTRIBUTING RESERVOIR.
ENGINE HOUSE.

D

Engines and Machinery.
Conduit.
Receiving Reservoir.
Open Canal and Connections with Streams.
Supply Reservoirs.
Distribution.

It is proper to remark, as a preliminary to this description, that these works are projected under peculiar natural features.

The character of the streams proposed to be used, their relative and remarkably low levels at surface, with reference to the mean high tide of the ocean, require a line of work of limited grade; which is determined at one end by the tide level, and at the other, for the present supply, by the low surface of L. Cornwell's Pond, including a distance of about 14 miles.

DISTRIBUTING RESERVOIR.

By examination of the general map accompanying this Report, it will be observed that the level of the shore on the northern side of the island is separated from that of the southern side, by a line of elevated land, which—in the City of Brooklyn—breaks down abruptly to the water's edge, from an elevation of 92 feet, forming the picturesque "Heights" of the City, and which continues thence easterly through the length of the island. Its longest "water-slope," or slope of descent, is on the southern side of this ridge. At a point on this summit ground, near the line of Fulton Avenue, and about five miles from the City Hall, a natural depression occurs peculiarly suited for a reservoir, where it is possible, without very great cost, to construct distributing reservoirs, covering with their appurtenances, an extent of 47 acres, with a surface elevation of 172 feet above mean tide, as determined by a line five feet below the coping of the United States Dry Dock. In fitness of purpose, central location, elevation, and economy of construction, this is the most advantageous point for such reservoirs on the western end of the island.

In the plans herewith submitted, provision is made for dividing the Reservoir into three apartments. The first may have a surface area of 17 acres, and a depth of 20 feet, to be used as a Settling Reservoir, into which the engines will discharge; the second is to take its supply from the surface of the Settling Reservoir, and to be used as a Supply Reservoir, with a surface area of 6 1-2 acres, and a depth of 20 feet; and the third to take its supply from the surface of the second, with a surface area of 6 1-2 acres, and a depth of 20 feet; to connect immediately with the distribution main. It is believed that there is favorable ground in the immediate vicinity for the construction of other reservoirs should they ever be required.

The division walls and gate houses of these apartments are so arranged, that either, or all, can be used for distribution, and either may be drawn down and cleaned through a sewer connected with a ravine in the immediate vicinity. These apartments jointly will be capable of supplying to the City five millions of gallons daily, for at least forty days, in the event of accident or stoppage to the machinery or line of conduit; which would be at the rate of 25 gallons per day each, for a population of 200,000 souls.

The plans of the Reservoir include the iron railing, fencing, and turfing, in connection with the carriage road through the grounds, with two ornamental carriage entrances, and keeper's house, and one large gate-house at the junction of the several apartments, together with the smaller influx and efflux chambers. A wall of rubble and rock-dressed masonry, surmounted by an ornamental coping, will be built on the line of the Cypress Hill Plank Road, along the northern side of the Reservoir.

ENGINE HOUSE.

At the terminus of the conduit in the deep excavation, near the Long Island Railroad, it is proposed to construct the engine house and pump well.

As the grade of the pump well is unavoidably governed by the level of the receiving and supply reservoirs on the line, its foundations must be built below the level of mean tide.

Under these circumstances, and in view of the character of the excavation, plans have been prepared for a foundation of rectangular form 100 feet long by 37 feet wide, built in the most substantial manner of rubble masonry, with one inverted arch, sustained by heavy abutments, the whole resting on piles of 12 inches diameter, with cap timbers 12 inches square, filled in with concrete masonry, and covered with a plank floor six inches deep firmly tree-nailed down.

With these foundations, which are carried up to the level of the engine-room floor, the pumping machinery is connected, so as to relieve the walls of the building from vibration.

The pump well is constructed in two divisions. The first receives the supply from the conduit, and the second is built parallel with it, and contains four separate pump chambers, so arranged by division walls and gates as to connect them, or shut off either from the others, for purposes of cleaning, repairs of valves, &c., &c.

These gates will be worked from the floor of the pump well room, below the engine room floor, which connects with the floor of the boiler room on one side, and the air chamber room on the other, both being below the water-table of the engine room, for greater convenience in the manner of arranging the steam pipes, and other details of the machinery.

The area covered by these several rooms will be 103 feet long by 100 feet in width.

The main building which contains the engine room, will be 100 feet long by 60 feet wide, and 64 feet high to the peak of the roof. It will be constructed in the modern Italian style: the lower portion of the building on three sides being faced with the valuable "Magnesian Marble," recently introduced into this market, with rusticated corners, door and window-jambs, door and window-caps, and sills, belt course, and water-table of the same material.— The upper portion of the building will be of brick, presenting that contrast in color which is a peculiar and elegant feature in this style of structure. The main entrance to the building will be 14 feet wide by 16 feet high. The roof will be of galvanized tinned corrugated iron, supported on wrought iron, trussed principals and purlines.

ENGINES AND MACHINERY.

The large amount of daily supply proposed for the City, the location of the engine house relative to that of the distributing reservoir, and the elevation to which the supply must be raised, require that the pumping machinery designed for this work should be of the most substantial, effective, and economical kind.

From the day of the first practical steam engine, described by the Marquis of Worcester, in his "Century of the Names and Scantlings of the Marquis of Worcester's Inventions," published in 1663, and the engine of Thomas Savary of 1698, down to the days of Smeaton and Watt, and from that time to the present day; the efficiency of the steam engine, which was first called into use for the purpose of pumping water, has attained its maximum in the same employment.

The extensive and varied experience furnished on this peculiar application, has shown in practice, what is also readily demonstrated in theory, that the single acting counterbalance beam engine, commonly known as the Cornish Engine, working under high pressure, with a large ratio of expansion, a slow motion, and a long stroke, combines the most simple and perfect mechanism for the elevation of water into extensive reservoirs.

Without dwelling on this subject, I have simply to remark that uniformity of motion is by no means necessary for a pumping engine. The steam valves must open gradually, and the velocity of the piston must increase from the commencement of its stroke, and gradually diminish at the end of the stroke. This reciprocating motion is relieved under a given amount of work, by a long stroke of piston in preference to a short one; the process of expansion is more perfect; no sudden reaction is brought on any of the working parts, and the action of the pump is also more complete in its upward as well as downward stroke, the water which it lifts having a better opportunity to fill the vacuum caused by its upward motion.

The following table of the comparative performance of single and double acting engines, will more fully illustrate my views on these points.

	Diameter of Cylinder.	Length of stroke.	Number of Strokes per minute.	Pressure per sq. inch above or below the atmosphere.	Ratio of expansion on stroke.	Weight in ft. lbs. raised by 112 lbs of Coal.
Atmospheric Engine, Long Benton, Northumberland,	52 in.	7 ft.	12	0.00	0.00	12.600.000
Double Acting Engine, Albion Mills,	34 "	8 "	16	2.50	0.00³	25.756.752
" " " Congleton, Cheshire,	13 "	4 "	27.5	20.00	0.00	12.418.560
Single " " East London, Water Works,	79 3-4	10 "	7.	5.17	0.687	105.664.118
" " " Holmbush,	50	9.1 "	4.63	30.00	0.833	140.484.848

With these views the engine room has been arranged for two single-acting engines, each of 12 feet stroke, and 80 inches bore of cylinder, each capable of elevating 10,000,000 of gallons daily, with provision for two additional engines of the same size, when the increased wants of the City require more than twenty millions daily supply.

The calculations of dimensions, duty, &c., of one of the Cornish engines, designed for the Brooklyn Water Works, by Samuel McElroy, C. E., February, 1854 are as follows:

Supply of Engine to Reservoir, 10,000,000 galls. (N.Y.) per 24 hours.
Elevation of Reservoir above Tide, ... 172 feet.
Lift of Plunger, 7' to 19'—average 13 feet.
Reservoir Surface above av'g lift line, 172'—20',5=151,5.
Quantity=115,74 gals. per sec.=6944,4 gals per minute.
    = 6944,4 ÷ 7,8   = 890,3 c. ft. " "
    = 6944,4 × 8   =55.555,2 lbs. " "
    = 55.555,2 × 166,'25   =9.236,051,6 ft. lbs. raised.
    = 55.555,2 × 151,5   =8.416.612,8 " " forced.
Stroke of Piston and Plunger, =12 feet.
Number of effective strokes, =10 per minute.
Diameter of Cylinder, =80 inches.
Area,   "   " 80^2 × ,7854=5026,64 sq. inches.
Diameter of Plunger,   =37",8.
890,3 c. ft. ÷10=89,03 c. ft. per stroke—add 5 per cent for loss of action=89,03 + 4,45 = 93,48 c. ft. required capacity.

$\frac{93,48}{12}$ = 7,79 sq. ft. $\sqrt{\frac{7,79}{,7854}}$ = $\sqrt{9,92}$ =3',15=37",8 diam.

Pump pressure = $\frac{151,5 \times 15}{33}$ = 68,86 lbs. per square inch;

Add friction of force tube:
$p = \frac{q^3 l}{140 d^5} = \frac{115,74^3 \times 63.360}{140 \times 36^5} = \frac{1.550.442,95 \times 63.360}{140 \times 65.131.776} = \frac{98.236.065.312}{9.118.448.640} = 11\ H.P.$ =11 × 33.000 =

363.000 ft. lbs. = 0,43 per cent. on amount forced;—add for friction of check valves, ,017 per cent. = ,06 per cent. 68,86 + ,06 per cent. = 68,86 + 4.14 =73,00 lbs. per square inch. Total resistance, 7,79 × 144 = 1121,76 × 73 = 81888 lbs. ÷ 2000 = 40,94 tons. Pressure on piston (mean), =73 lbs. (plunger pressure), + 20 per cent. for friction of engine = 73 + 14,6 = 87,6 lbs. per square inch, equivalent; then 5026,64 : 1121,76 :: 87,6 : 20 lbs. per square inch required on piston.

DUTY OF ENGINE.

Water.	9.236.061 ft. lbs.
Friction of Force Tube, ...	504.996
" " Engine, ...	1.683.322
Total, ...	11.424.379 ft. lbs.
Actual Horse Power, ...	346

The plans for the machinery contemplated at present, include two air chambers, with copper caps and lining, 12 feet in diameter, and 19 feet high, each connecting with a line of 36 inch force tube, provided with check valves, flanges, and other necessary appurtenances, and entering the settling Reservoir at the Influx Chamber.

CONDUIT.

From the pump well to the receiving reservoir, at Baiseley's Pond, a conduit will be constructed, of the following dimensions:—

Breadth of base,	15 feet.
External height,	10 " 8 inches.
Internal width,	10 "
" height,	8 " 8 "
Water area (for 40,000,000 gallons discharge)	50 square feet.
Water perimeter for do.	30 feet.
Grade, per mile,	6 inches.

The flow of this conduit, when running five feet deep, will be 40,000,000 gallons daily, as calculated by the formula of Weisbach—

$$h = z + \frac{l\,p}{F} + \frac{c^2}{2g}. \text{ where}$$

h = fall.
l = length in feet.
q = quantity in cubic ft. per sec:
F = water area.
p = " perimeter.
c = velocity in feet per sec:
g = acceleration of gravity.
z = coefficient of friction.

The foundations of the conduit will be laid on concrete masonry, where the ground is sufficiently firm, which will rest on a dry rubble wall where the ground requires it.

The hanch walls will be of rubble masonry, 30 inches wide at the base, and 20 inches at the top, with a lining of brick masonry four inches thick. The bottom of the conduit will be an inverted arch of 18 feet radius in brick masonry resting on the concrete foundations. From the hanch walls a semicircle of brick masonry of five feet radius (internal), and 12 inches thick, will form the top of the conduit, with spandrel backing of brick masonry, as shown more fully on the accompanying plans.

The back filling in embankment will be four feet above the extrados of the upper arch, eight feet wide at top, with side slopes of one and a half to one.

Ample provision is made on this line for the necessary creek and box culverts, waste weirs, ventilators, man-holes, &c.

The Conduit will connect with the influx gate-house at the receiving reservoir.

RECEIVING RESERVOIR.

For a reservoir of storage as well as supply, it is proposed to move the present dam of Baiseley's Pond southerly, and to increase its height 7 1-4 inches so as to flood about ninety acres.

The whole water perimeter of the pond will be thoroughly grubbed and cleaned. An ornamental roadway will be constructed around its banks, with bridges over the three inlets on the northern side. An influx chamber of masonry will be built for the entrance of the open canal from the east, and a gate and keeper's house on the southern side at the connection with the conduit.

OPEN CANAL AND CONNECTIONS WITH STREAMS.

From the storing reservoir, the several supply ponds proposed to be used will discharge into an open canal.

The comparatively slight grade which the open canal will require, taken in connection with its economy of construction, the cost otherwise involved by raising the several ponds at the eastern end of the line, and its retired location, are some of the reasons recommending it to your favorable consideration.

West of Simonsons' Pond the canal will have a breadth at base of prism of 7 1-2 feet, with internal side-slopes of 1 1-2 to 1, the depth of prism will be six feet, the width of berme-banks five feet—with embankment and excavation slopes of one and a half to one. The water perimeter of the prism will be lined with puddling 12 inches thick. In excavation berm drains will be constructed two feet wide and one foot deep, to prevent the surface water from entering the canal; and these drains will discharge into the box culverts, or waste-weirs, at convenient points.

The several ponds intended to be used as supply reservoirs, east of the storing reservoir, are Nostrand's, Simonson's P. Cornwell's, Pine's, L. Cornwell's, and Smith's.

These will be connected with the main canal line by lateral canals of similar construction to the main line, with the dimensions, grades, efflux and influx chambers, and other structures required.

The flow of the main canal, west of Simonson's, when running five feet deep, will be 35,000,000 gallons daily, as determined by the formula above quoted; the grade being two inches per mile. The grade line to which the levels are referred, is the bottom line of the water-way.

East of Simonson's Pond, the cross section of the prism will be reduced in width, according to the several reductions in supply, to maintain the same grade and depth, agreeably to the plans herewith submitted, and in view of ultimately using the supply of Willis', Jones', Smith's, and Massapequa Ponds.

The road and farm bridges, waste-weirs, box culverts, and other mechanical structures, on this portion of the work, will be in masonry and superstructure of a substantial and ornamental character.

SUPPLY RESERVOIRS.

Of these ponds contiguous to the line of work, five are to be used as supply Reservoirs, and for this purpose are to be thoroughly grubbed and cleaned. New dams are to be erected on each, of the form and dimensions shown on the accompanying plans, with aprons of masonry. As will be noticed on the general plan of dam and apron, the line of puddle-wall is continued unbroken the entire length of the embankment, and protected at the apron by an arch of brick masonry. Provision is also made in the gate-chamber for draining the pond at any time.

As these ponds derive their principal supply from bed-springs, there can be no doubt that their present discharge will be largely increased by grubbing and clearing their beds.

DISTRIBUTION.

For the present supply of the city, it is believed that eighty-five miles of distributing mains and pipes will suffice. These have been arranged with the following lengths and dimensions:—

5 Miles	36 inch	Pipes with	5	Stop-cocks,
1 "	30 "	"	2	"
2 "	20 "	"	2	"
12 "	12 "	"	50	"
30 "	8 "	"	70	"
30 "	6 "	"	70	"
5 "	4 "			

and 800 Hydrants with suitable drains.

These pipes will be laid through the graded streets designated by the Water Commissioners, not less than 3 1-2 feet below grade, with all the requisite joints and fixtures.

AGGREGATE OF ESTIMATES.

Distribution,	$1,434,311,58
Distributing Reservoir,	580,653,48
Engine House, &c.,	535,709,14
Conduit,	712,695,98
Canal,	176,133,32
Receiving Reservoir,	268,706,00
Supply " No. 1	29,245,48
" " " 2	40,520,62
" " " 3	45,699,40
" " " 4	201,325,00
Total,	$4,025,000,00

E

In conclusion, permit me to say that there are several features in this plan particularly advantageous.

Among these, are the large extent, favorable location, and economy in cost of the distributing reservoir.

This part of the work, when completed agreeably to the plans, will also be an attractive resort, as it commands one of the finest landscape and ocean views on that portion of the island. The buildings, entrances, and grounds, will all be of an ornamental character.

The relative position of the receiving and supply reservoirs on the line, and the system of construction, partly in conduit, and partly in open canal, is a feature peculiar to this work, regulated by the circumstances of supply and discharge. By this means, for more than one half the distance, the expense of a heavy conduit in masonry is avoided, and a large amount of expenditure is saved.

The great capacity of the conduit is a third characteristic peculiar to this line. Its internal width at the spring of the arch is two feet seven inches greater than that of the Croton Aqueduct, the cross-sections being similar in form, and when running but five feet deep, it will not pass less than 40,000,000 gallons per day.

Another feature peculiar to this plan, is that of the pumping machinery. This is arranged on a scale larger than any before designed for water-works in this country, and only equalled in a few cases in the experience of Europe. The four engines which will be eventually used on these works, will be placed side by side in an engine room 100 feet long by 60 feet wide. In detail of arrangement they will combine the benefits of the mining and pumping experience of Europe since 1698, which experience is as conclusive to the general plan adopted of single-acting, counter-balance engines. Although not heretofore introduced in this country in connection with water-works, except in the case of the Jersey City Water-Works, on which this form of engine has been adopted, though not yet in operation, they are most earnestly recommended.

If one of these engines can be constructed in time, I am of the opinion that a partial supply may be introduced into the city within fifteen months from the time of commencing the work. It will be impossible, however, to complete the works, as a whole, with due regard to their proper construction and finish, in less than two years.

I take great pleasure in making my acknowledgments to Samuel McElroy, Esq., Civil Engineer, for very valuable assistance in preparing the maps, plans, specifications, and estimates herewith submitted.

PLAN.

WHEREAS, the plan hertofore adopted by the Common Council to supply this city with water, and submitted to the electors thereof in July last, was not approved by them; And, whereas, the Common Council are by the act hereafter mentioned, authorised to submit other plans to said electors,

Therefore, Resolved, That the Common Council of the City of Brooklyn in pursuance of an act of the Legislature, entitled "An act for the supply of the City of Brooklyn with water," passed 3d June, 1853, do hereby provisionally adopt a plan for such supply, of which the following is an outline:

The sources from which the water will be obtained, are Parsonage Creek, Pine's Creek, Hook Creek, Jamaica Creek, and intermediate streams, which have been, or may be hereafter purchased for said purpose, and which are estimated to furnish twenty-three millions of gallons daily. The analysis of the water which has been made, shows it to be purer than that supplied to any other city in the country, Boston only excepted.

Suitable dams, or reservoirs, will be constructed on said streams, and the water will be brought to Baiseley's pond, in the town of Jamaica (as a receiving and settling reservoir), in an open canal, and thence by conduit to a point near the base of the hills, known as the Cypress Hills, where the pump-wells will be located, and the necessary steam engines and machinery erected to elevate the water to a reservoir to be located upon the summit of said hills, on land formerly of Isaac I. Snediker and Isaac Snediker, and lying partly in the town of New Lots, Kings County, and partly in the town of Newtown, Queen's County, which reservoir will be of ample capacity to contain a supply of at least two hundred millions of gallons of water, and from thence the water will be distributed by pipes throughout the city, as the wants of the citizens and the location of the population may require.

The conduit and canal will be constructed of suitable capacity to carry forty millions of gallons of water to the pump-wells.

The estimated cost of bringing from the farthest point named, a sufficient supply of water for the present wants of the city, including the cost of streams, land, damages, canal, conduit, pump-wells, steam engines and machinery, reservoirs, eighty miles of distribution pipes, eight hundred hydrants, and all other things necessary to complete the work in the best manner, is four millions five hundred thousand dollars.

It is estimated that the supply thus obtained will be sufficient for the population of four hundred thousand inhabitants, allowing fifty gallons daily to each one.

The additional cost for a population of eight hundred thousand will consist of such further steam power as may be necessary to elevate the additional quantity of water which may be required, and of such further distribution pipes as may be necessary to furnish the same to the consumers, and the expense of continuing the canal eastward, and purchasing some of the streams beyond.

DOCUMENT NO. TWO.

SPECIFICATIONS

FOR THE

BROOKLYN WATER WORKS.

ACCOMPANYING REPORT

OF

THE WATER COMMITTEE OF THE COMMON COUNCIL;

MADE

MARCH 13th, 1854.

———•••———

ALD. JOHN A. DAYTON,—*Chairman.*
GEN. WARD B. BURNET,—*Chief Engineer.*
SAMUEL McELROY,—*Principal Assistant Engineer.*

SPECIFICATIONS.

1st.—General.
2nd.—Grubbing, Chopping, and Clearing.
3rd.—Excavation.
4th.—Embankment.
5th.—Puddling.
6th.—Mortar.
7th.—Masonry.
8th.—Iron Work.
9th.—Composition Work.
10th.—Painting.
11th.—Distribution.
12th.—Distributing Reservoir.
13th.—Engine House.
14th.—Engines and Machinery.
15th.—Conduit.
16th.—Receiving Reservoir.
17th.—Canal.
18th.—Supply Reservoirs.
19th.—Mechanical Structures.

BROOKLYN WATER WORKS
GENERAL SPECIFICATIONS.

Articles of Agreement, made and concluded this   day of   1854.
Between
*   of the City of Brooklyn. Party of the First Part, and*
*   Party of the Second Party ; whereby*
it is covenanted and agreed as follows :—

The said party of the second part, hereby agree that they will furnish all the materials (which shall be sound, durable, and of the best quality for the purposes required), and all the tools necessary, and perform all the labor necessary, to construct and finish, in the most workmanlike and substantial manner, the Brooklyn Water Works, consisting of :

An open canal from Smith's pond to Baiseley's pond, with its appurtenances ;

A covered conduit from Baiseley's pond to the engine-house and pumpwell, with its appurtenances ;

A line of force tubes from the engine-house to the distributing reservoir, with its appurtenances ;

A distributing reservoir in three apartments with its appurtenances ; and

A system of City distribution, commencing at said reservoir, embracing 80 miles of distribution pipe, with its appurtenances.

The construction of said work shall be in all respects according to the specifications, and to the maps and plans hereto attached, numbered from 1 to   inclusive, and approved by the Party of the First Part, and subject to the direction and approval of the Chief Engineer, appointed by the said Party of the First Part, who shall be in charge of the work, which shall be at all times subject to his inspection. He shall decide all questions relative to the proper execution of the work under the aforesaid specifications, maps, and plans, provided that in case of any difference in opinion with the Party of the Second Part, involving a cost exceeding two thousand dollars; they shall have a right to appoint an Engineer on their part, both Engineers forming a Board, which in case of disagreement, shall appoint a third Engineer, both forming a Board, whose decision by a majority shall be final; the expenses of said Board to be borne by said Party of the Second Part.

It is further agreed, that in case unforeseen circumstances should render any change ad-

F

visable in the plans for the mechanical structures or line of works, such changes may be made with the mutual consent of the parties to this agreement.

It is also agreed, that on the 1st day of each and every month after the commencement of said works, the Chief Engineer shall make and return an estimate of the amount and *pro rata* value of the work done by the Party of the Second Part, under this agreement, on which estimates' payments shall be promptly made to them, receiving   per cent of the amount due and unpaid, which reservation shall be held by the Party of the First Part, as a guarantee for the faithful performance of this agreement.

In case of the absence or inability to act of the Chief Engineer, the Principal Assistant Engineer shall be vested with the powers herein conferred on the Chief Engineer.

And it is further agreed, that the said Party of the Second Part shall convey to the said Party of the First Part, all the right, title, and interest of the Long Island Water Works Co., to the ponds and streams, lands and reservoir grounds, held by said Co. under its charter; and shall guarantee to the Party of the First Part, a supply of water for distribution by the construction of the works herein named, of not less than twenty million gallons of water daily.

GRUBBING CHOPPING, AND CLEANING.

For the ground required to be occupied by the excavations and embankments; for the conduit, canal, and reservoirs; for the culverts, side drains, protection walls, bridge abutments, road crossings, and other structures pertaining to the Water Works; all trees, saplings, bushes, roots, wood and perishable materials, shall be removed and burnt up, or otherwise disposed

The ponds used for the supply of the canal or conduit, must also be cleared of all vegetable and perishable matter below their flow line, as determined by the height of their several dams.

In the removal and disposition of such material, care shall be taken that no damage is incurred to the land or property adjoining those taken for the work.

EXCAVATIONS.

All necessary excavation and removal of earth, sand, stones, and other materials, buildings and other structures, shall be made for the construction of the Conduit, canal, reservoir, engine-house, ponds, drains, bridges, culverts, drains, road-crossings, permanent and temporary drains, waste-weirs, ventilators, gate-houses, and other mechanical structures pertaining to the work.

The excavations for the foundations shall be made to the proper depth and form for said foundations, the earth being carefully cut and prepared by ramming or otherwise for the same. Where the conduit and canal are in embankment, and foundation walls are necessary, proper excavations for the same shall be made. In the excavations shoring and plank for their protection from caving shall be provided and placed. Under the embankments the soil shall be removed to a proper depth. The excavations shall progress with the general work, and be so made as to avoid unnecessary damage to property along the line. The best material procured from the excavations shall be appropriated to the embankments and back filling, the surplus earth being deposited in spoil banks of proper form and height.

All materials found in the excavations suitable for the various parts of the work adjacent, shall be used where required. Under this head all pumping, bailing, and draining to keep the work free from water, while the mechanical structures are building, shall be performed in the most effective manner.

EMBANKMENT.

All the proper embankments required for the construction of the several parts of the work, shall be made of proper and sound material, with such slopes, and method of construction as required by the approved plans for the same.

The foundations for the embankments shall be prepared as described under the head of Grubbing, Chopping, &c.," and "Excavation."

In forming the embankments, care shall be taken to raise them by successive layers, sloping towards the centre of the bank, with other necessary precautions to prevent slips. On the embankments for the dams, the width at top shall not be less than 15 feet, with side slopes of two horizontal to one vertical; on the canal, the width of berm shall be 6 feet, without side and inside slopes of 1 1-2 to 1, and for the road crossings, abutments, and other structures, the same slope shall be maintained, except where specially provided for herein on the approved plans, or by the requirements of particular portions of the work during its progress.

Where puddling, masonry, &c., are connected with the embankments, care must be taken to adapt one part of the work to the other, in order to insure the perfection of the whole.

The material shall be taken from the nearest excavation suitable therefor, or in case of no adjacent suitable excavations, from "borrowing pits," to be provided for the same, of convenient access. Previous to the completion of the work, the embankments shall be properly turfed or seeded, where it is necessary to prevent their washing by rain or otherwise.

Under this head will be included all necessary "back filling" for the several portions of the work. The back filling for the conduit shall be four feet in depth, over the extrados of the arch, eight feet wide at top, with slopes of 1 1-2 to 1; it shall not be done until the mortar and plastering is laid, and shall be put on in a regular and even manner, and be rammed as it is laid. The back filling for other portions of the work, shall be adapted to their several requirements.

PUDDLING.

In the construction of the dams, canal, division walls and other portions of the work where puddling is required, the earth used for this purpose, shall be of proper quality, and shall be worked in thin layers, each of which must be thoroughly wet and tempered, and worked so as to incorporate each course with its adjacent course. Care shall be taken to carry on this work in a connected manner, to prevent checks, and to ensure its tightness The dimensions of the puddle walls in length and section, shall be in accordance with the plans approved for the work.

MORTAR.

All the Mortar used on this work, must be made of the best quality of ground hydraulic lime, which shall be subject to proper and sufficient tests of its freshness and strength.

In wet work it shall be made of equal parts of cement and sand, and in other places, of two parts sand to one of cement—the proportions being ascertained by careful measurement. Care must be taken to protect the cement from the weather, previous to its use. The sand shall be free from impurities and coarse grained. It shall be properly screened before its use.

In mixing Mortar, the cement and sand of the required proportions, shall be first mixed dry, and then wet to a proper consistency, and used while fresh. Where grout is required, it must be mixed as above described, and kept in brisk motion after it is made liquid, until it is used.

MASONRY.

Concrete Masonry, shall be made with mortar as above described, by adding thereto five parts of durable broken stone or gravel to each part of cement, and thoroughly mixing and incorporating the mass.

The concrete stone or gravel, shall not exceed 2 1-2 inches in diameter, and shall be cleaned from dirt, &c. The material thus prepared shall be immediately laid in the place intended for it; care being taken to avoid throwing it from an elevation, and to sustain it by the natural ground slope in preference to moulds, where this can be conveniently done. After laying it must be rammed, until the mortar "flushes" to the surface. Where the bed of concrete exceeds 12 inches in depth, it must be formed by successive layers, to the proper height, each not more than 12 inches deep.

Dry Rubble Masonry, shall be made of sound durable stone, quarried out in regular beds Where laid in foundation walls, protection walls, abutments and other structures of the work, the stone must have a proper area of bed, with a thickness of not less than four inches, the broadest and best bed shall be always laid down, the bed joints being made up by suitable spalls, and the vertical joints filled in with the same. The wall shall be well tied with headers in a substantial bond.

Rubble Masonry shall be laid with stone of the quality above described, and in similar manner. The spalls for the beds of the stone, together with the stone, being laid in a full bed of mortar. Where required, the vertical joints shall be grouted or filled with mortar the chaps and spalls being put in afterwards.

The stone shall be clean, and always wet before they are laid; no dressing or hammering to be done after the stone are laid.

DRESSED MASONRY, required for the culverts, waste weirs, ventilators and other structures, shall be laid with a joint not exceeding 3-8 of an inch. The top and bottom beds shall be squared for a depth not less than 15 inches; the end joints to be squared for a depth not less than 9 inches. The face of the stone shall be made with a tool draft around the arris, or dressed in the same manner as the beds; the first being designated as "rock-dressed," and the second as "dressed" masonry. Where the dress of the face is not specially mentioned herein, or noted on the approved plans, it shall be "rough hammered."

The work shall be laid up in regular courses, with a suitable bond in front, and with headers equal to one-fourth the face stone.

CUT STONE. The jambs, corners, coping, caps and other portions of the mechanical structures required to be of cut stone, shall be properly cut and fitted in mortar to their respective places with the necessary grooves and checks, the large stone being lewised and set by machinery. The quality of the material to be in all respects according to the approved plans, and suitable for the work.

BRICK MASONRY. The bricks used in the conduit, and other structures not exposed to sight after the completion of the work, shall be of the best quality of hard burnt brick; those used for face-work of buildings, ventilators, &c., must be of the best quality of face brick—equal to those known in market as the Colougburgh brick. They must be selected before they are laid, and the smoothest and best laid in the face of the work. They must be well soaked before laying, and laid with a good bond in a full bed of mortar. In arches the bed shall be laid in the radius line, with uniform joints, and alternate header and stretcher courses, where the arch exceeds 4 inches in thickness. Where the brick work shows, and on the inside of the conduit, the joints shall be jointed with a tool.

No masonry shall be laid on the work during weather sufficiently cold to injure the setting of the cement.

IRON WORK.

All the cut and wrought spikes, nails, straps, bolts, nuts, rods, valves and other appurtenances and materials of wrought iron, required for the work, with all the cast iron appurtenances required, are to be furnished and fitted in their proper places, and to be of suitable quality for the several parts of the work, as required by the general and detailed plans and directions aforesaid, and the progress of the work.

COMPOSITION WORK,

For the lining of the valves, bearings, valve-seats, and all other metal work on the several structures required to be of composition, the same shall be furnished of proper quality and dimensions, and accurately secured and fitted to their proper places, agreeably to the plans and directions aforesaid, and in accordance with the progress of the work.

PAINTING.

On the completion of any portion of this work, so far as to require painting for its protection, the iron and metal work, inside work, and other parts, shall have two sufficient coats of peroxide of zinc paint, properly mixed and laid of the color designated by the Chief Engineer: the fences, and such other portions of the work as he may designate being covered with two coats of white or other wash, prepared to stand the weather.

DISTRIBUTION.

Through such graded streets of the City of Brooklyn as may be directed by the Engineer the distributing pipes connecting with the Distributing Reservoir, shall be laid of the following sizes, dimensions and lengths.

    5 Miles Pipe 36 inches diameter,
    1 " " 30 " "
    2 " " 20 " "
    12 " " 12 " "
    30 " " 8 " "
    30 " " 6 " "
    5 " Hydrant 4 " "

The top of said pipes to be laid not less than 3 1-2 feet below the grade line; the trenches to be excavated to a sufficient width and depth for this purpose; and the pavement carefully replaced at grade on the back filling.

These pipes are to be provided with all the necessary side joints and fixtures, and are to be tested with a pressure of 300 lbs. per square inch, to the satisfaction of the Engineer.

The system of distribution will also be provided with the following appurtenances placed under the direction of the Engineer.

    800 Hydrants with proper and sufficient drains.

    5 36 inch stop cocks,
    2 30 " "
    2 20 " "
    50 12 " "
    70 8 " "
    70 6 " "

adapted in size to the size of distribution pipe to which they are to be connected.

DISTRIBUTING RESERVOIR.

On the high ground at Cypress Hill provided for the site of the Distributing Reservoir, there shall be constructed a Reservoir, having a surface elevation of 172 feet above mean tide as determined by a line 5 feet below the coping of the United States Dry Dock, Brooklyn Navy Yard.

Said reservoir shall be divided by proper division walls into 3 apartments having a surface area of 17, 6 1-2, and 6 1-2 acres respectively. To be provided with a proper influx chamber for the force tubes from the engines, and a proper and sufficient Gate House for draining all the apartments which shall be connected with waste pipes and gates for this purpose, and for which a proper sewer shall be provided to the ravine at the foot of the hill :—and with a distribution well common to the three divisions, so that either or all may be used for distribution.

Division weirs, chambers, and appurtenances shall be provided for the connections of each apartment.

The surface to be covered by said Reservoir and its appurtenances, shall be about 47 acres. The depth of the apartments to be 20 feet. The embankments to be 20 feet wide at top, with side slope of 2 and 3 feet to one. The apartments to be lined with concrete 12 inches deep to a point 2 feet above the water level, covered with a brick flooring 4 inches thick.

The buildings connected with the Reservoir to consist of one Gate House and one Keeper's House, with stone foundations, brick walls, with windows, doors, and other appurtenances, and two carriage entrances, built according to the plans and directions above mentioned.

The grubbing and clearing to be performed agreeably to the foregoing specifications.

On the Cypress Hill Plank Road, a wall of rubble and rock dressed masonry will be built to sustain the Reservoir bank, with a coping course, and an iron railing, and with a section, and dimensions agreeably to the plans and directions aforesaid. Fences, roadways, turfing and ornamenting the grounds, will also be done agreeably to the same.

All the work on the Reservoir aforesaid to be in all respects according to the foregoing specifications and plans, and under the directions of the Chief Engineer.

ENGINE HOUSE.

The Engine House with its appurtenances shall be built with a pump well, boiler room, air chamber room and engine room.

The excavation for the pump well shall be made to a point 18 feet below the surface level of the conduit; the foundations of said well being 100 feet long by 44 feet wide, and constructed on round spruce piles of 12 inches diameter at the butt, placed 3 feet from centre to centre both ways, and about 30 feet long, or long enough to be driven to a uniform guage of one inch at the last blow. When the piles have been driven and cut off at the proper level, cap timbers of 12 inches square shall be treenailed on them with yellow pine or locust, 2 1-2 inch treenails, and the intermediate spaces filled in with concrete masonry flush with the top of said timbers, and 18 inches deep, worked in firmly around the heads of the piles. On said timbers, hemlock plank 6 inches thick, of good quality and free from sap shall be treenailed with two inch treenails, on which courses of rubble dressed masonry shall be built to a height of 16 feet along the line of well with an inverted arch of 10 feet radius as shown on the plans aforesaid. On the rubble masonry, piers and walls of brick, and marble (dressed) masonry hollow or solid, as shown on the plans, shall be built with such openings, arches and dimensions as required by the plans aforesaid. Brick division walls shall also be provided with openings and dimensions as shown, by which the pumps of each engine will work in a separate well, which may be shut of from the wells adjacent if required.

The floor of the Pump Well Room shall be supported on white pine beams 4 inches by 12 inches, as drawn, on which 2 inch merchantable white pine plank shall be firmly nailed. Provision shall also be made on this floor for working the several well gates, and for preventing, as far as possible, the evaporation of the well from affecting the machinery in the Engine-Room.

The Boiler Room floor shall be on the same level with the Pump Well floor, as shown on the plan, the internal dimensions to be 96 feet long by 32 1-4 feet wide. The foundation of the side and end walls, except the side wall which supports the Engine-Room, &c., to be of rubble masonry 4 feet high, 40 inches broad at top and 48 at bottom, resting on foundation plank, and a double row of round piles as drawn. A foundation wall for the boilers to be provided, resting on a plank foundation. The chimney attached to this room to have a foundation in common with the Engine-Room wall, and to be carried up with it, the section of the flue being 36 inches square, with a vertical height of 79 feet. The foundation to rest on 12 piles 12 inches diameter at the butt, about 30 feet long, and driven to a one inch guage, with 6 × 12 inch cap timbers, tree-nailed down, and filled in with concrete 12 inches deep. The side and end walls to be of brick two feet thick as drawn.

The air chamber room floor will be on the level of the pump well room floor, and will be 96 feet long by 15 feet wide (internal dimensions), the side and end wall foundations, together with the foundations of the air-chambers, will be of rubble masonry, resting on a grillage of plank and timber, and concrete as drawn. The end and side walls will be of brick, 24 inches thick, the roof being formed of a series of arches, 12 inches thick as drawn.

The engine-room will be built with internal dimensions of 96 feet long, by 56 feet wide and 49 feet high to the top of the wall, the front and end walls will be 24 inches thick, with a facing of "magnesian marble" or "steatite," in courses of 3 and 5 inches thick, alternately to a point, 20 feet above the water table, thence the walls will be of brick, 20 inches thick, the offset being made on the outside as drawn. The water table, courses, lower windows, doors, belt course, window caps and sills, will be ornamented with rustic blocks, cut, and levelled as drawn, of the magnesian marble. The rear wall will be of brick, with the same belt, course, and offsets as the other walls. The chimney will be carried to a height of 37 1-2 feet above the water table, with a cut stone cap as drawn,

The roof will be laid on a "quarter rise" of galvanized tinned, corrugated iron, No. 20 guage, supported on wrought iron, trussed principals and purlines, the principals being not more than 12 feet apart.

The cornice shall be made of brick, with an upper number of "magnesian marble," as drawn, the rain and water shall be conveyed from the roof by galvanized iron conductors, at each corner of the building of 5 inches diameter.

All the work on the engine house and its appurtenances to be in all respects according to the specifications, maps, and plans, and the directions aforesaid.

ENGINES AND MACHINERY.

Two steam pumping condensing engines, shall be erected in the engine room, on the foundations previously prepared for them, each with a cylinder of 12 feet stroke, and 80 inches bore, and a plunger pump, with a plunger of 12 feet stroke, and 37 8-10 inches diameter. These engines are to be provided with firm cast iron and cut stone frames, properly secured to the building, and to be provided in every respect with the valve chests, condensers, air pumps, force pumps, bearings, stuffing boxes, connecting rods, guides, bolts, nuts, oil cups, and all other appurtenances necessary. To have working beams, 36 feet long between centres and counter-balances, attached to the plungers, adjustable to different loads. Each engine is to be provided with two boilers, properly built of "boiler plate" iron, with all the steam and water gauges, man-holes, plates, grate bars, safety valves, and other appurtenances necessary, with sufficient steam-generating power to enable each engine to raise into the distributing reservoir ten millions of gallons of water per 24 hours.

The iron and composition work, surface work, and finished work, in dimensions and arrangement to be, in all respects, according to the plans for the same, and the directions aforesaid.

All the valves, valve shafts, bearings, gates, stop cocks, flanges, bolts, nuts, screws, and all other parts of machinery required for the works, to be made of wrought or cast iron, or composition, of the best quality, for the purposes required, and according to the plans and directions aforesaid.

Each part and piece of said engines and machinery to be subject to the inspection of the Engineer, during its construction or after it is in place, and to be thoroughly tested as to its fitness for use and durability, when complete and in its proper place. Under this head will be included two force tubes of 36 inches diameter each, laid from the connections with the air-chambers to the influx chamber of the distributing reservoir, with all the flanges, joints, check-valves, bolts, nuts, and other appurtenances, and laid on the line and grade designated on the maps and plans, and under the directions of the Chief Engineer.

All the work on the above to be according to the specifications, plans, and directions aforesaid.

CONDUIT.

The grubbing, chopping and clearing, and excavations for the foundations of the conduit shall be made agreeably to the foregoing specifications. Where the natural ground is sufficiently compact for the same, a foundation of concrete masonry, 15 feet wide, shall be laid, and prepared to receive the abutments, and inverted arch, of the forms and dimensions given in the plans. Where a plank and timber dry wall, or piled foundation is required under the concrete, the same shall be carefully made according to plans and specifications aforesaid. On the concrete foundation thus prepared, abutment walls of rubble masonry, 30 inches wide at bottom, and 20 inches wide at the spring line of the upper arch, shall be built up in uniform height, to prevent irregular settling, after which, an inverted arch of brick masonry, 4 inches thick, and with a radius of 18 feet, shall be turned between said abutments, resting on a full bed of mortar. A lining of the same thickness shall also be made to the abutments, to the spring line of the arch, and well secured to the same. From the top of the abutments, a semicircle of brick masonry, of 5 feet (internal), radius shall be turned, 12 inches thick, with spandal backing of brick masonry, agreeably to the plans. The internal dimensions of said culvert to be 8 feet 8 inches from the intrados of the inverted arch to the intrados of the upper arch, and 10 feet wide at the spring line of the upper arch, the side linings having a batir of two inches. The least thickness of the concrete foundations to be 8 inches.

The centering for the arches to be accurately constructed for the same, with proper ribs of plank, and secured by wedges so as to strike the centering after the completion of the arch.

At such points on the line of conduit as may be designated, man-holes (not exceeding 20 in number), shall be made 3 feet in diameter, built up to the top of back filling, with cut ring stones of proper form, per plans, and covered with flag stones 5 inches thick, with iron rings properly secured to the same. Cess pools shall be built in the conduit, under the same, where required.

The back filling, embankments, &c., shall be made agreeably to the foregoing specifications and plans, together with all the influx and efflux chambers, connecting gates, gate-houses foundations, and other portions of mechanical structures required. The location, line and grade of said conduit with all its structures being built according to the maps and directions aforesaid.

The grade line of the conduit will be the intrados of the inverted arch, at the centre of the same.

RECEIVING RESERVOIR.

The pond known as Baiseley's Pond, shall be properly grubbed, cleared, excavated, and formed, agreeably to the foregoing plans and specifications, for permanent use, as a Receiving Reservoir, by the construction of a stone dam and apron, and other works agreeably to the plans for the same. Said Reservoir to have a surface area of not less than 92 acres, with 9 feet depth of water-way, and to be provided with a proper influx chamber for the line of canal from the west, as per plans. Provision shall also be made at the apron, for draining down the reservoir to admit of thoroughly cleaning the same.

The structures to consist of a stone dam, gate and keeper's house, apron, influx chamber, and a carriage road not less than 12 feet wide around the entire flow-line of said reservoir enclosed with an ornamental and substantial fencing.

The surface level to be 9 feet above Mean tide, and the contents 250,800,000 gallons.

CANAL.

From the receiving reservoir there shall be constructed a line of open Canal, eastward to the connection with P. Cornwell's pond, with all the grubbing, &c., excavations, embankments, puddling, &c., agreeably to the plans and specifications for the same. West of Simonson's pond, the canal will have a breadth at base of 7 1-2 feet, with side slopes of one and a half horizontal to one vertical, a side lining of puddling 12 inches thick being made, (agreeably to the specifications for the same), around the water perimeter, as per plans. The berm banks of said canal to be 7 feet high above grade, 6 feet wide at top, with side slopes of one and a half to one, and with berm drains three feet wide, and one foot deep in excavation, to prevent the surface water from entering the canal, said drains to discharge at convenient points in the box culverts, or waste-weirs, as per plans. The grade line of said canal to be the bottom line of the water-way, and the grade to be two inches per mile. The canal to be capable of passing, when running 5 feet deep, 35 million gallons water daily. East of Simonson's, the canal will be constructed in the same manner with reduced dimensions in width, as required by the reduction in its supply, to maintain the same grade and depth, according to the plans and directions for the same.

All the road, and farm bridges, waste-weirs, and culverts, connections with ponds, and lateral canals, and other structures required, to be made agreeably to the plans and specifications aforesaid.

LATERAL CANALS.

In order to connect the supply Reservoirs with the line of the canal aforesaid, the beds of the streams which now constitute their outlets, shall be thoroughly grubbed, excavated, mucked, and embanked, from the aprons of said Supply Reservoir Dam to the canal, with a water section adapted in and grade to the maximum flow of the outlet.

At the junction with the canal, a suitable dressed stone bulkhead shall be constructed across the line of the lateral canal so as to raise its level to that of the water in said canal. Said bulkhead to be provided with two composition gates, adapted to openings 3 feet high by 2 feet wide, suitably arranged for feeding the canal. On the canal-bank opposite the bulk-head a waste-weir shall be built to provide for any surplus discharge.

From the upper face of the bulk-head to the lower face of the waste-weir, a pipe of 24 inches internal diameter shall be laid, below the grade level of the canal, provided with a proper stop-cock, which can be used as a discharge line for the lateral canal, in case of repairs to the main canal. To provide for such repairs, bulk-heads and folding gates shall be placed across the main canal, at points contiguous to the entrance of the lateral canals.

Similar provision shall be made for taking in such additional streams on the line as may be designated.

SUPPLY RESERVOIRS.

These shall be four in number.

Number one being the pond known as Nostrand's Pond.
" two " " " " Simonson's "
" three " " " " P. Cornwell's "
" four " " Ponds " Smith's, Pine's and L. Cornwell's Ponds.

The Reservoirs thus designated to be properly grubbed, cleared, mucked, and otherwise prepared; all the old buildings, dams, &c., being removed as directed.

The structures for each to consist of a gate and keeper's house, a dressed stone apron, an earth dam, a surrounding carriage road, not less than 12 feet wide, substantial and ornamental bridging for such roads as are now legally established public-roads, and a substantial ornamental fencing around the property purchased for said Reservoirs.

The area and capacity of said Reservoirs to be as follows:

	Area.	Capacity.
Supply Reservoir No. 1.	10.25 acres.	24.250.000 gall's.
" " 2.	12.00 "	24.500.000 "
" " 3.	25.00 "	59.000.000 "
" " 4.	144.75 "	344.500.000 "
	192.00 "	452.250.000 "

The entire work to be performed agreeably to the plans and specifications aforesaid.

MECHANICAL STRUCTURES.

All the grubbing, excavations, embankments, masonry, iron and composition work, and wood work, painting, &c., &c., required for the

Gate House at the Distributing Reservoir.
Keeper's " " " " " "
Carriage Entrances " " " "
Influx Chambers " " " "
Division Wiers " " " "
Engineer's House   Engine House,
Rail Road, Turn Table and Side Track,
Ventilators on the Conduit,
Waste Wiers " " and Canal,
Road Crossings " "
Farm " " "
Creek Culverts " " " "
Box " " " " "
Road Bridges " " " "
Frame " " " "
Dams, Aprons " " Supply and Receiving Reservoirs,
Gate and Keeper's Houses, " " " " "
Influx and Efflux Chambers, " " " " "
Bulk Heads,   Canals,

with all other structures required, shall be constructed in form, materials, and method, according to the plans, specifications and directions aforesaid.

DOCUMENT, NO. THREE.

ESTIMATES OF COST

IN DETAIL.

BROOKLYN WATER WORKS,

1854.

ESTIMATE FOR CITY DISTRIBUTION

FROM DISTRIBUTING RESERVOIR.

5 miles 36 inch pipe laid,				$425,000
1 " 30 " "				68,000
2 " 20 " "				82,100
12 " 12 " "				172,000
30 " 8 " "				322,500
30 " 6 " "				240,000
5 " 4 " Hydrant				33,000
800 most approved patent Iron Hydrants placed, $30				24,000
8 stop cock for 36 inch pipe at $600 each.				4,800
2 " 30 " 500				1,000
4 " 20 " 250				1,000
60 " 12 " 100				6,000
80 " 8 " 60				4,800
80 " 6 " 50				4,000
Labor and implements for proving pipes				46,111,58
		Total,		1,434,311,58

DISTRIBUTING RESERVOIR.

35 acres Grubbing and clearing $1,00			$3,500,00
245,410 yds Embankment	15c.		36,811,50
153,122 " Excavation,	12c.		18,374,64
43,870 " Concrete,	$7		307,090,00
8,754,368 Hard Bt. Brick,	$650		56,903,34
2,286 yds. Rock dressed masonry,	9		20,574,00
1,400 feet Cut stone Coping,	175		2,450,00
1,400 " Iron railing,	5		7,000,00
4,100 " Fencing,	25c.		1,025,00
800 " Efflux culvert,	$30		24,000,00
	Carried Forward,		$477,728,98

Brought Forward,		$477,728,98
1,500 feet Drainage Pipe, 36″ $16		24,000,00
800 " Distribution Pipes, 36″ 16		12,800,00
6 Stop Cocks for do. do.		3,000,00
6,500 feet Carriage Roads, 25c.		1,625,00
1 Influx Chamber complete,		8,000,00
3 Connecting Weirs "		18,000,00
1 Gate House, "		16,000,00
2 Carriage Entrances, "		6,000,00
Turfing Banks, &c.,		1,500,00
Keeper's House,		12,000,00
Total,		$580,653,48

ENGINE HOUSE.

18,311 c yds Excavation,	25c.	$4,577,50
Bailing and Draining,		25,000,00
671 Piles (driven),	$10	6,710,00
32,516 ft. Bm. Capping, 25c. ft.	40	1,300,64
300 c yds. Concrete,	9	2,700,00
3,420 " Dressed Masonry,	12	41,040,00
635 " Cut Stone,	16	10,160,00
1,150 " Brick,	10	11,500,00
1,350 square yards Plastering,	1	1,350,00
5,948 square feet marble front,	1	5,948,00
644 feet " water table,	150	966,00
390 " " Cornice,	250	975,00
48 Window Caps,	4	192,00
48 " Sills,	3	144,00
84 Rustic Blocks,	1,50	126,00
Corrugated Roof,		14,000,00
84 Iron Window Sashes,	20	1,680,00
6 " Doors,	230	1,380,00
60 " Floor Beams,	80	4,800,00
8 " Cylinder "	250	2,000,00
5,200 square ft. Iron Flooring,	1,75	9,100,00
Influx Chamber,		4,000,00
2 Cornish Engines (complete,)		160,000,00
2 Air Chambers, "		6,000,00
Engineer's House, &c.,		8,000,00
Fencing (Iron,)		9,500,00
Railroad (turnout, &c.)		4,000,00
11,760 feet Force Tubes, 36 inches diameter, $16		188,160,00
12 Check Valves and Connections,		10,400,00
Total,		$535,709,14

CONDUIT.

28 acres Grubbing and Clearing,	$100	. .	$2,800,00
22,250 cub. yards Mucking,	30c.	. .	6,675,00
344,212 " Excavation,	18c.	. .	61,976,16
276,711 " Back Filling,	12c.	. .	33,205,32
Bailing and Draining,	.	. .	15,000,00
2,000 feet Piling,	$15,30	. .	30,600,00
600 cub. yards Dry Masonry,	6,00	. .	3,600,00
13,600 " Concrete (laid,)	8,00	. .	108,800,00
16,270 " Masonry,	9,00	. .	146,430,00
23,106 " Brick (with centering,)	10,25	. .	248,389,50
13,600 square yards plastering,	50c.	. .	6,800,00
51,000 feet Fencing,	12c.	. .	6,120,00
5 Ventilators (Complete,)		. .	5000,00
50 Man Holes,	100	. .	5,000,00
38 Farm Crossings,	80	. .	3,040,00
15 Road Bridges,	120	. .	1,860,00
8 Creek Culverts,	2,050	. .	16,400,00
1 Waste Weir (spring creek,)	.	. .	6,000,00
Temporary Road and Bridges,	.	. .	5,000,00
Total,			$712,695,98

CANAL.

40 acres Grubbing and Clearing,	$100	. .	$4,000 00
24,400 cub. yards mucking,	30c.	. .	7,332 00
334,830 " excavation,	15c.	. .	50,224 00
26,261 " embankment,	12c.	. .	3,151 00
76,600 feet fencing,	12c.	. .	9,192 00
18 Road Bridges,	$1,650	. .	29,700 00
33 Farm "	900	. .	29,700 00
5 Waste Weirs,	650	. .	3,250 00
4 Bulk Heads,	575	. .	2,300 00
4 Creek Culverts,	2,050	. .	8,200 00
5 " Bulk Heads,	600	. .	3,000 00
Bailing and Draining,	.	. .	15,000 00
Turfing Slopes,	.	. ,	1,500 00
19,167 cub. yards Puddling,	50c.	. .	9,583 50
Total,			$176,133 32

H

RECEIVING RESERVOIR.

47 Acres Grubbing and Clearing,	$100	$4,700 00
593,520 cub. yards Mucking,	30c.	178,056 00
9,800 feet Carriage Road,	10c.	980 00
650 " Bridging,	15	9,750 00
850 " Stone Dam,	74	62,900 00
11,000 " Fencing,	12c.	1,320 00
Gate and Keeper's House,		4,000 00
Influx Chamber (Canal,)		1,000 00
Removing Buildings and Dam,		6,000 00
Total,		$268,706 00

STORING RESERVOIR—No. 1.

5 acres Grubbing and Clearing,	$100	$500 00
33,072 cubic yards Mucking,	30c.	9,921 60
2,378 feet Carriage Roads,	10c.	237 80
4,884 " Fencing,	12c.	586 08
30 " Bridging,	15	450 00
240 " Earth Dam,	20	4,800 00
2,750 " Lateral Canal,	1	2,750 00
Gate House, &c.,		4,000 00
Removing Buildings and Dam,		6,000 00
Total,		$29,245 48

STORING RESERVOIR—No. 2.

5 acres Grubbing and Clearing,	$100	$500 00
58,043 cub. yards Mucking,	30c.	17,412 00
3,300 feet Carriage Roads,	10c.	330 00
4,356 " Fencing,	12c.	522 72
231 " Bridging,	15 00	3,465 00
277 " Earth Dam,	20 00	5,540 00
2,750 " Lateral Canal,	1 00	2,750 00
Gate and Keeper's House,		4,000 00
Removing Buildings and Dam,		6,000 00
Total,		$46,520 72

STORING RESERVOIR—No. 3.

8 acres Grubbing and Clearing,	$100		$800 00
80,670 cub. yards Mucking,	30c.		24,201 00
6,204 feet Carriage Roads,	10c.		620 40
6,400 " Fencing,	12c.		768 00
30 " Bridging,	15		450 00
343 " Earth Dam,	20		6,860 00
2,000 " Lateral Canal,	1		2,000 00
Gate and Keeper's House,			4,000 00
Removing Buildings and Dam,			6000 00
Total,			$45,699 40

STORING RESERVOIR—No. 4.

40 acres Grubbing and Clearing,	$100		$4,000 00
464,270 cub. yards Mucking	30c.		139,281 00
16,600 feet Carriage Roads,	10c.		1,660 00
18,002 " Fencing,	12c.		1,784 00
1,200 " Bridging,	15		18,000 00
1,430 " Earth Dam,	20		20,600 00
Gate and Keeper's House &c.,			4,000 00
Removing Buildings and Dams,			12,000 00
Total,			$201,325 00

SUMMARY OF ESTIMATES.

Distribution	$1,434,311 58
Distribution Reservoir	580,653 48
Engine House	535,709 14
Conduit	702,695 98
Open Canal	176,133 32
Receiving Reservoir	268,706 00
Storing " No. 1	29,245 48
" " 2	40,520 62
" " 3	45,699 40
" " 4	201,325 00
Total,	$4,025,000 00

DOCUMENT, NO. FOUR.

REPORT

OF

SAMUEL M^CELROY,

PRINCIPAL ASSISTANT ENGINEER,

ON THE

FINAL LOCATION,

OF THE

CONDUIT AND CANAL LINE,

BROOKLYN WATER WORKS.

Brooklyn, May, 1854.

Sir:

I have the honor to report that the final location of the line is now complete, from the dam at Smith's Pond to the influx chamber at Baiseley's Pond for the Canal; from the Gate House at Baiseley's to the Engine House for the Conduit; and from the Engine House to the Distributing Reservoir on Cypress Hill for the Force Tubes.

A test level has also been carried from the coping of the United States Dry Dock to the bench mark at Baiseley's, intersecting the benches of the conduit line at the Engine House, and continued thence to the bench on Cypress Hill. In checking the level notes by a return line, the difference at the Dry Dock was found to be eight thousandths of a foot, so slight as to verify the benches for all practical purposes.

In the curves on the centre line I found no difficulty in adopting a uniform radius, viz: that of nineteen hundred and ten feet, or three degrees per one hundred feet chord, and the stations are made accordingly.

By the information acquired from previous surveys, more particularly those of Daniel Marsh and Thomas T. Wierman, Esquires, made under your direction, I have been enabled to combine the most direct and easy line with a proper regard to economy in earth work, and to complete the location in a short time, although it is for the most part on new ground.

In this duty I have to express my acknowledgements to Messrs. John Houston and Alexander McElroy, Assistants in charge of the field parties, for the prompt and accurate manner in which their duties have been discharged.

I append a description in detail of the line staked out, with other statements connected with the work.

Respectfully Submitted,
SAMUEL McELROY,
Principal Assistant Engineer.

GEN. WARD B. BURNETT,
Chief Engineer
BROOKLYN WATER WORKS.

DESCRIPTION OF CONDUIT LINE.

Commences at the location of the Engine House, on the Western side of the Long Island Railroad, at the head of Spring Creek valley, and runs thence on a curve of 1,910 feet radius 500 feet; thence N. 25° W. 927 feet; thence on a curve of 1,910 feet radius 533 feet; thence N. 41° W. 3,767 feet; thence on a curve of 1,910 feet radius 733 feet: thence N. 65° W. 5,200 feet; thence on a curve of 1,910 feet radius 600 feet; thence N. 8° W. 2,234 feet; thence on a curve of 1,910 feet radius 865 feet, thence S. 73° W. 1,300 feet; thence on a curve of 1,910 feet radius 900 feet; thence N. 80° W. 3,200 feet; thence on a curve of 1,910 feet radius 1,200 feet; thence S. 64° W. 2,400 feet; and thence 215 feet to the Gate House at Baiseley's Pond.

The total length of line being	. .	24,615 feet.
" " tangents,	. .	19,283 "
" " curvature,	. .	5332 "

The grade line which is the bottom line of the water way of the conduit, is at the Pump Well, 2 feet above mean tide water, thence to Spring Creek level, and thence to Baisley's Pond, on an inclination of 6 inches per mile, being at said Gate House, 4 feet above mean tide water.

DESCRIPTION OF CANAL LINE.

Commences at the Influx Chamber at Baisley's Pond, and runs thence N. 70° W. 7,620 feet; thence on a curve of 1,910 feet radius 500 feet; thence N. 85° W. 9,600 feet; thence on a curve of 1,910 feet radius 700 feet; thence N. 64° W. 3,050 feet; thence on a curve of 1,910 feet radius 300 feet; thence N. 55° W. 7,390 feet; thence on a curve of 1,910 feet radius 1,433 feet; thence S. 82° W. 6,021 feet; thence on a curve of 955 feet radius 1,416 feet; and thence 304 feet to the efflux gate of Supply Reservoir No. 4.

The total length of line being	. .	38,334 feet.
" " tangents,	. .	33,985 "
" " curvature,	. .	4,349 "

The Grade line of the canal, which is the bottom of the water-way, is at the Receiving Reservoir, 4 feet above mean tide; and at the Storing Reservoir No. 4, 5,22 feet above mean tide; the inclination being at the rate of 2 inches per mile.

STATEMENT OF RESERVOIR SURFACE AND CAPACITY.

Distributing Reservoir,	. .		30 acres.	. .	200,000,000 galls.
Receiving "	. .		92 1-4 "	. .	250,800,000 "
Supply, "	. No. 1		10 1-4 "	. .	24,250,000 "
" "	. " 2		12 "	. .	24,500,000 "
" "	. " 3		25 "	. .	59,000.000 "
" "	. " 4		144 3-4 "	.	344,5000,00 "
Total,			314 1-4 acres.		903,050,000

PARTY EMPLOYED ON FINAL LOCATION.

GEN. WARD B. BURNETT,	*Chief Engineer.*
SAMUEL McELROY,	*Prin. Assist. Engineer.*
JOHN HOUSTON,	*Assist. Engineer.*
ALEXANDER McELROY,	*Assist. Engineer.*
GEORGE H. MERRILL,	*Rodman.*
ALBERT C. DEMERITT,	*Rodman.*
STEPHEN R. HUDSON,	*Chainman.*
JOHN D. MARTIN,	*Chainman.*
JOHN T. DAYTON,	*Flagman.*

DOCUMENT NO. FIVE.

LIST OF MAPS AND PLANS

BROOKLYN WATER WORKS.

Map No. 1.—General Map.
    2.—Distribution Pipe.
    3.—Conduit Line, Sheet, No. 1.
    4.—   "   "   "   2.
    5.—Canal   "   "   3.
    6.—   "   "   "   4.
    7.—   "   "   "   5.
    8.—Distributing Reservoir.
    9.—Receiving   "
    10.—Supply   "   No. 1.
    11.—   "   "   2.
    12.—   "   "   3.
    13.—   "   "   4.

Plan No. 1.—Keeper's House, Distributing Reservoir.
    2.—Gate   "   "   "
    3.—   "   "   "   "   Plan.
    4.—Carriage Entrance,   "   "
    5.—Engine House, Elevation.
    6.—   "   "   Plan and Section.
    7.—Pumping Engine.
    8.—Dam and Apron.
    9.—Road Bridge, Canal.
    10.—Farm   "   "
    11.—Creek Culverts.
    12.—Box   "
    13.—Waste Weir, Conduit.
    14.—   "   "   Canal.
    15.—Sections, Conduit and Canal.
    16.—Gate and Keeper's House.

DOCUMENT, NO. SIX.

PROPOSITION

OF

H. S. WELLS AND CO

FOR THE

CONSTRUCTION

OF THE

BROOKLYN WATER WORKS.

To
      JOHN A. DAYTON, ESQ., *Chairman of the Water Committee,*

SIR,

  We propose to construct the Water Works for the City of Brooklyn complete, according to the plans and specifications of the Engineer of the City, and subject to the approval of the Water Commissioners to be appointed; and to convey to the City of Brooklyn all the real estate and streams of the Long Island Water Works Company, including the Reservoir site, for Four Millions One Hundred and Seventy-Five Thousand Dollars, and guarantee a daily supply of Twenty Millions of Gallons of water daily; and making said works a capacity of double that amount.

                                      Respectfully,
                                              Your Obedient Servant,
                                                  H. S. WELLS & CO.

March 6th 1854.

DOCUMENT, NO. SEVEN.

REPORT

OF THE

WATER COMMITTEE,

SUBMITTING THE

CORRESPONDENCE WITH THE

LONG ISLAND WATER WORKS COMPANY.

REPORT

OF THE

WATER COMMITTEE,

SUBMITTING CORRESPONDENCE WITH THE

LONG ISLAND WATER WORKS COMPANY.

COMMON COUNCIL.

REGULAR MEETING.

MONDAY, May 1, 1854.

Present—Aldermen Holt, Merrill, Brainard, Barnard, Fowler, Mulligan, Remsen, Graham, Jackson, Wyckoff, Oliver, Campbell, Hinman, Dayton, Hooper, and White.—Alderman Wilson presided.

The minutes of the stated meeting of the 24th, and also of the special meeting of the 27th ult. were read and approved.

The Water Committee, on resolution of the Common Council, on the 27th of March last, relative to a negotiation with the Williamsburgh Water Works Company with a view to purchase the interest, property and effects of said Company, reported—

That in pursuance of the direction of the Common Council, they addressed a letter to the Long Island Water Works Company, which is the name of the Company formerly called the Williamsburgh Water Works Company, and subsequently another to H. S. Welles, & Co., the parties referred to in the answer of the President of that Company—which letters and the answers thereto are annexed to this report.

Mr. Dean, the President of the Company, states that the Company had agreed to convey all its water rights and grounds, to the City of Brooklyn, upon the request of Henry S. Welles & Co., in the event of their being able to conclude a contract for building the works, " and that pending this negotiation, the Long Island Water Works Company are not at liberty

K

to enter upon a new arrangement." Messrs. Welles & Co. in their answer, state that they had made a proposition to the City, to construct the Water Works Complete, and the vesting of the entire property of the Company in the City, which proposition was made as a whole, and does not admit of a division.

The report of this Committee, submitted to this Board on the 13th of March last, presented substantially the facts which the present inquiries have more specifically elicited. It was there stated that responsible parties had offered to build the water works for the city, at the estimates of the Engineer, and to vest the title, the property, and the privileges of the Long Island Water Works Company in the city, guaranteeing at the same time the supply of water from the sources proposed, to equal twenty millions of gallons a day. Those parties were Henry S. Welles & Co., above named. Before those gentlemen could make the offer which they did, it was necessary for them to obtain the right which was conceded to them by the Long Island Water Works Company. It was therefore impossible for the Company to negotiate with the City for its property, until that proposition was disposed of.

The Committee are, however, enabled to answer some of the points of the resolution referred to them, so far as regards the property of the Company, and the aggregate price paid for it in case the offer of Messrs. H. S. Welles & Co. should be accepted.

This property is stated in the letter of Mr. Dean, annexed to the report of this Committee submitted to the Common Council on the 27th of March, to consist of the following land and streams:

1. Reservoir Ground on Cypress Hills, of about 48 acres.

2. Baiseley's ponds and pondage land and mill.

3. Simonson's pond and pondage land and mill.

4. L. Cornwell's pond, grist and saw mills, with land flowed by pond.

5. Willis' pond, land and paper mill, for which property Messr. Welles & Co. have agreed to pay the Company upon the transfer of the title to the City, free from all incumbrances whatsover, the sum of one hundred and fifty thousand dollars.

All of which is respectfully submitted.

JOHN A. DAYTON,
D. P. BARNARD,
R. C. BRAINARD, } Water Committee.
F. G. QUEVEDO,
SAMUEL BOOTH.

Brooklyn, May 1, 1854.

The following is the correspondence alluded to in the report:—

[COPY.]

Brooklyn, April 24, 1854.

Dear Sir:

The Water Committee of the Common Council having been authorized to open a negotiation for the purchase of the various lands and streams owned by the Long Island Water Works Company, would request that you would, at the earliest moment, inform the Committee whether the Company wish to sell the property mentioned in your note dated 27th of March last, if so, please give us the price for each parcel or in one sum for the whole property mentioned.

Your obedient Servant,

JOHN A. DAYTON,

Chairman Water Committee.

To Nicholas Dean, Esq.,

President of the Long Island Water Works Company.

No. 45 Merchant's Exchange,
New York, April 28, 1854.

Dear Sir:

Your letter, enquiring on behalf of the Water Committee, upon what terms the Long Island Water Works Company would dispose of their property, of which a statement was furnished to you in my letter of the 27th March last, is received.

From the moment of my connection with the Company above named, I have always been impressed with the belief that the works through which your city is to derive its supply of water, should be constructed by, and owned and controlled by the city itself. This opinion I have constantly maintained to my colleagues, and all others, when the subject has been discussed; it is my *unalterable opinion.*

Interests of such vast magnitude now, and in the future, so intimately blended with the health and daily comforts of your citizens; so important in protecting property from the devastations of fire, should never be left within the control and management of any power outside of the municipal government of the city. The difficulties inherent to any other mode have often been felt in cities; they are now felt to an insufferable degree in London, and to a considerable extent in Baltimore. In every case of a conflagration the interests of the company, and those of the city, are directly antagonistic; the one would limit the supply of water to the smallest possible quantity, while the other requires it *ad libitum.*

Acting under these convictions, this company has agreed to convey all its water rights and grounds to the City of Brooklyn, upon the request of the firm of Henry S. Welles & Co. eminent contractors, in the event of their being able to conclude with its government a contract for building the works.

Pending this negotiation, the Long Island Water Works Company are not at liberty to enter upon a new arrangement.

Very truly and respectfully, Yours

NICHOLAS DEAN,

President.

John A. Dayton, Esq., Chairman,

Water Committee, Brooklyn.

[COPY.]

Brooklyn, April 26th, 1854.

Messrs. H. S. Welles & Co:

Gentlemen :

The Water Committee of the Common Council having been authorised to open negotiations for the purchase of the various lands and streams owned by the L. I. Water Works Co., being informed that you now have the control of the same, would request that you would at the earliest moment inform the Committee upon the subject as set forth in the annexed resolution, which was passed by the Common Council, And oblige.

Your Obedient Servant,

JOHN A. DAYTON,

Chairman Water Committee

New York, April 27th, 1854.

Hon. John A. Dayton, Chairman Water Committee :

Yours, covering a resolution of the Common Council of the City of Brooklyn, of the 27th of March last, and requesting an answer thereto, has been received.

In reply we have to state that in order to enable us to make a full and satisfactory proposition to construct the Water Works of the City of Brooklyn, we sought and obtained from the Long Island Water Works Company, the right to require a conveyance of its lands, reservoir grounds, streams and pondage grounds to the City of Brooklyn, in case our proposition should be accepted. That proposition was made and is now before the Honorable the Common Council and the Public, and embraces the construction of the whole works complete, and vesting of the entire property of the Company in the city. It is therefore evidently impossible for us to separate the one from the other; the proposition is made as a whole. We invite the severest scrutiny of that proposition, satisfied that it will be a saving of millions of dollars to your city, over any other plan yet suggested.

Respectfully, Your Obedient Servants.

H. S. WELLES & CO.

The Water Committee to whom was referred the annexed resolution of Ald. Fowler.

Respectfully report that they have addressed the following letter to the President of the Long Island Water Works Company.

BOOKLYN, March 28d, 1854.

To Nicholas Dean, Esq.,

President of the Long Island Water Works Company.

DEAR SIR:

The Common Council of this city have adopted the accompanying resolution to which I beg, (by direction of the Water Committee) to direct your attention, and to request an answer to the inquiries therein proposed.

Your Obedient Servant,

JOHN A. DAYTON.

Chairman of the Water Committee.

Your Committee have received the annexed reply, and recommend that the papers be placed on file, and the Committee be discharged from further consideration of the subject.

JOHN A. DAYTON,
F. G. QUEVEDO,   } Water Committee.
D. P. BARNARD,

Amended "that the Water Committee is hereby directed to open a negotiation with those duly authorised on behalf of the Williamsburgh Water Works Company, for the interest, property and effects of said Company, to ascertain in detail what the said Campany offers for sale—the price of each item offered for sale, as well as the price in the aggregate—and report the same to this Board in writing—with a view that this Board may determine how far the interest of the City of Brooklyn, as relates to the introduction of water, may require the purchase of the interest, property, and effects of the Williamsburgh Water Company."—Adopted by unanimous consent.

March 27th, 1854.

JOSEPH HEGEMAN, Clerk.

Approved March 29, 1854.

EDWARD A. LAMBERT, Mayor.

[COPY.]

In Common Council,
March, 13th, 1854.

By Ald. Fowler—*Resolved*, That it is hereby referred to the Water Committee to make the necessary enquiry of those duly authorised on behalf of the Williamsburg Water Works Co., of the terms and conditions on which said Company proposes to sell its interests, property and effects, and report the same in writing to the Common Council for its consideration, with a specification of what said Company offers for sale.—Adopted.

Joseph Hegeman, Clerk.

Approved March 15th, 1854.

Edward A. Lambert, Mayor.

Office of the Long Island Water Works Co.,
No. 45 Merchants Exchange, N. Y.
March 27th, 1854.

Dear Sir:

In reply to your inquiry I state that no application has ever been made, to my knowledge, by or from the City of Brooklyn, or any of its officers, to purchase the water rights and franchises of this Company.

Individuals, who are understood to have been negociating with Brooklyn for furnishing it a supply of water, have suggested to this Company a desire to purchase them out, but I am not aware that these suggestions have resulted in any definite or fixed arrangement.

At the foot I give you a brief detail of the property now held by this Company, to which these negociations related.

Very respectfully, sir, yours,

Nicholas Dean, President.

Alderman Dayton, Chairman, &c.

1st.—Reservoir Grounds on Cypress Hills, about 48 acres.

2d.—Baiseley's Pond, Jamaica Creek, and Pondage Land, with Mill, &c.

3d.—Simonson's Pond, Hook Creek, Mill and Pondage Land.

4th.—Cornwell's Pond, Parsonage Creek, Grist and Saw Mills, with Lands flowed by Pond.

5th.—Willis' Pond, East Meadow Creek, Paper Mill and Land.

Ald. Dayton, moved that the Report be accepted and placed on file, which was decided in the affirmative; ayes 17, nays 5.

DOCUMENT NO. EIGHT.

OUTLINE OF PLAN

FOR

SUPPLYING THE CITY OF BROOKLYN WITH WATER;

ADOPTED MAY 11TH, BY

RESOLUTION OF THE COMMON COUNCIL,

AND

SUBMITTED TO THE ELECTORS,

JUNE 1st 1854.

Whereas, the plan heretofore adopted by the Common Council to supply this city with water, and submitted to the electors thereof in July last, was not approved by them, and whereas, the Common Council are by the act hereafter mentioned, authorised to submit other plans to said electors. Therefore—

Resolved,—That the Common Council of the city of Brooklyn in pursuance of an act of the Legislature, entitled, "An Act for the supply of the city of Brooklyn with water," passed 3d June, 1853, do hereby provisionally adopt a plan for such supply, of which the following is an outline :

The sources from which the water will be obtained, are Parsonage Creek, and intermediate streams, which have been, or may be hereafter purchased for said purpose, and which are estimated to furnish twenty three millions of gallons daily. The analysis of the water which has been made, shows it to be purer than that supplied to any other city in the country, Boston only excepted.

Suitable dams or reservoirs will be constructed on said streams, and the water will be brought to a receiving and settling reservoir in the town of Jamaica in an open canal, and thence by conduit to a point near the base of the hills known as the Cypress Hills, where the pump-wells will be located, and the necessary steam engines and machinery erected, to elevate 20,000,000 gallons of water daily to the reservoir to be located upon the summit of said hills, which reservoir will be of ample capacity to contain a supply of at least 200,000,000 of gallons of water, and from thence the water will be distributed by pipes throughout the city, as the wants of the citizens and the location of the population may require.

The conduit and canal will be constructed of suitable capacity to carry 40,000,000 of gallons of water to the pump wells, and the construction of the entire works to be given out in one

L

or more contracts as shall be deemed most conducive to public interest, provided that the whole expense of said works and property to be purchased, shall not exceed the sum of $4,500,000, the amount provided by law.

The contract shall be given to the lowest responsible bidder or bidders, who will give adequate security, to be approved by the Common Council.

The estimated cost of bringing from the farthest point named, a sufficient supply of water for the present wants of the city, including the cost of streams, land, damages, canal, conduit, pump-wells, steam engines and machinery, reservoirs, eighty miles of distribution pipes, eight hundred hydrants, and all other things necessary, to complete the work in the best manner, is four millions five hundred thousand dollars.

It is estimated that the supply thus obtained will be sufficient for a population of four hundred thousand inhabitants, allowing fifty gallons daily to each one.

The additional cost for a population of eight hundred thousand, will consist of such further steam power as may be necessary to elevate the additional quantity of water which may be required, and of such further distribution pipes as may be necessary to furnish the same to the consumers, and the expense of continuing the canal eastward, and purchasing some of the streams beyond.

DOCUMENT, NO. NINE.

REPORT

OF

JOHN S. STODDARD,

CITY SURVEYOR,

ON THE SUBJECT OF

SUPPLYING BROOKLYN WITH WATER,

BY THE

WELL SYSTEM.

Mr. John S. Stoddard, *Civil Engineer:*

Dear Sir:—Of late our citizens have been somewhat agitated upon the subject of a supply of water from wells; and a pamphlet has been published under the signature of our late worthy citizen, Jas. Walters, upon this subject; and the Water Committee of the Common Council being desirous to obtain full information upon every point connected with the subject, so as to enable them to satisfy the public mind of the true source, as to quantity and quality, as well as cost, respectfully solicit you, at your earliest convenience, to prepare for the Water Committee a statement of your views upon this important subject.

Your Obedient Servant,

JOHN A. DAYTON,

Chairman of the Water Committee.

REPORT.

BROOKLYN, May 15th, 1854.

To JOHN A. DAYTON, ESQ., *Chairman Water Committee:*

DEAR SIR:

I have received your's of the 6th instant, requesting me to present my views upon the plan of supplying the city with water from wells; and in reply, I have to state as follows:

Twenty millions of gallons per day have been assumed by the Common Council, and as I understand by the public, as the quantity which any admissible plan must provide for; and all my calculations are based upon that amount.

It is a remarkable circumstance that good wells can be had at any place on Long Island.

As a general thing the water does not seem to run in veins, or narrow subterranean streams, but the whole mass of the Island seems to be saturated with fresh water, from an unknown depth below tide, to a height varying from 1 foot to 20 feet, and in one case to 25 feet above tide.

This mass of saturated earth has been called the main spring of the Island. Its upper surface ascends constantly, though not regularly, from the shore towards the centre of the Island; and the levels of a great number of the wells indicate that its average elevation is eleven feet above tide.

It varies slightly with the seasons. In wet years it is higher than in dry years; but the variations are small, scarcely exceeding two or three feet from an average level;—and comparatively it may be considered permanent.

All our good wells penetrate this main spring to a greater or less depth, and derive their water from it. Wells which furnish a large amount of water, must of necessity drain a larger portion of the main spring than wells which furnish only a small quantity of water; and as it requires more power to force water two miles through the earth than to force it one mile, the water must be driven into larger wells, by a greater power than is required by small wells. It is a fixed principle that water will not run up hill, nor on a level, but that it always runs down hill. Water flowing naturally, invariably assumes a slope, which descends constantly from the source of the stream towards its discharge, or mouth; so that the surface of the water at any given point is always lower than it is at any point nearer the source, and higher than at any point nearer the discharge.

Where the water is confined in pipes or in veins, the case is somewhat different, but even then it is always true that a certain head of water is requisite to overcome the friction of a certain length of pipe.

If we apply the above principle to the case of our wells, we shall find that as our large wells draw from large districts, so that the water has to pass through longer distances than the water which comes into small wells; and as long slopes have more fall than corresponding short slopes, the large wells must be deeper than the small ones; and that, generally speaking, a well which drains a certain district of the main spring must be sunk a certain depth below the *surface* of the main spring. In fact, in order that a well may *exhaust* any portion of the main spring, it must be so deep that a line drawn upwards from the bottom of the well to the outside of the drainage district, will have the slope that is requisite to force the water through the earth, from the outside of the district to the well. If it requires a slope of 10 feet per mile to force the water through the earth, and the district extends one mile every way from the well, then the well must be 10 feet below the main spring in order to exhaust the district. If the well drains two miles, then the well must be 20 feet below the spring, and so on. Supposing the main spring to be uniformly porous, all the water that is above a line drawn upwards from the bottom of the well, and sloping outwards, at the rate of one mile for every 10 feet of rise, can be drawn into the well; and the water that is below this slope cannot be drawn into the well, because there is not sufficient head to force it through the earth.

It is perhaps impossible to ascertain what is the least slope per mile, that will enable water to percolate through the earth. But, it is not necessary to know that extreme limit, in order to calculate the probable yield of a well.

The supply must come in freely, and we want to know what is the slope that will be able to produce that supply every day, year by year; not what could fill the well once a week, or once a month.

As it requires a greater head to force water a great distance through the earth, than it does to force it through a short distance, and as this head can only be obtained by digging the wells deeper, the drainage district of every well is necessarily limited by the depth to which it is practicable to sink the well; and consequently, though the main spring may be inexhaustible as a whole, yet any portion of it may be so far exhausted as to dry the wells, provided it is not replenished.

For, as before shown, the drainage extends upwards and outwards, on a slope from the bottom of the well, to the top of the main spring; all the water that is contained in the earth above that slope, can be drawn into the well; and no more; or, what amounts to the same thing, it cannot be drawn in fast enough to do any good. The largest possible drainage district for any single well, is from salt water on one side of the island to salt water on the other side, because, if any well were to be pumped down so low, as to draw in salt water, it would be ruined.

As before stated, all our wells are sunk some distance into this main spring. Water naturally seeks to find its level, and if any well is undisturbed, the water in it will rise to the level of the main spring; and consequently, we can ascertain the level of the main spring by taking the levels of the wells.

This main spring receives every year, from various sources, a certain amount of water, and it also discharges every year a certain quantity of water, principally through springs. If it discharges more than it receives, it must evidently be lowered, from year to year; and if it receives more than it discharges, it will evidently rise from year to year; therefore, if for any considerable length of time, the surface of the main spring remains constantly at the same level, it is clear, that upon an average, it must discharge, just as much as it receives.

We know by our wells, that the surface of the main spring is remarkably constant, and consequently, that an equilibrium has been established, between the influx into the main spring, and, the efflux from the same, no matter what source the influx comes from.

This efflux, or drainage, from the main spring, passes through subterranean courses, into springs, and from these springs through streams into the ocean.

Each portion of the main spring discharges into some spring at a lower level; and as this discharge is equal to all the accessions to that part of the main spring, from year to year, it is evident that the surface of that part of the main spring has, in course of time, been raised up just high enough to gain the head that is necessary to force the water through the earth, from that place to the place of its discharge, as fast as it is received, from year to year.

If we knew where any particular portion of the main spring discharges itself, then, by measuring the distance between that point and the place of its discharge, and taking the difference of level between the surfaces of the water at the two places, we could ascertain, for that particular place, the head or slope per mile, that was necessary to force the water through the earth to the place of its discharge, as fast as it comes into that part of the main spring. And by ascertaining the slopes at various places, we could establish an average slope, which would be a fair basis of calculation.

The Island generally is so intersected by streams, that it is impossible to tell where the water comes from.

But if we take the district between Clason avenue and Bedford avenue, there can be no doubt that a large portion of it drains into the Wallabout. I have taken the levels of between 30 and 40 wells in that district, and on both sides of it.

The general range is pretty uniform, and the levels of Franklin avenue afford a fair average.

At Franklin and Flushing the water stands above tide 3 feet
    Willoughby avenue,   10 "
    Gates   "   13 "
    Fulton   "   14 "
    Wyckoff street,   15 "

The nearest discharging point for the Fulton avenue well is the Wallabout; and for the Wyckoff street well is Gowanus;—the distances and levels being very nearly the same.

The Wallabout discharge is, on an average, three feet above tide, and two hundred feet north of Flushing avenue.

The Fulton avenue well is about 11 feet above its discharge, and about one and one quarter miles distant.

The slope or head is rather less than 10 feet per mile; and the same holds of the Wyckoff street well.

The flow of water in this district has been considerably obstructed by filling in, and therefore, it may reasonably be considered that a slope of 10 feet per mile is sufficient, taking year by year, to drain off the surplus water of any portion of the main spring.

In establishing a plan for supplying twenty millions of gallons per day from wells, the first point to be settled is, how many wells there shall be? and the second point is, where shall they be placed?

Some persons have advocated a single well of great size; others have recommended a combination of smaller wells.

The first is advocated more particularly by those who consider the main spring to be inexhaustible. The second by those who trust to the yearly accessions to the main spring, and rely upon its surplus waters, without proposing to reduce the present contents of the main spring. All the wells, springs and streams upon the Island depend upon the main spring. It collects an immense quantity of water in wet seasons, and discharges it gradually in dry seasons. It is just high enough to force the water through the earth to the springs. If it were to be materially lowered it would dry up all the springs and wells, and be a serious public calamity. It was never intended to be drained, and any project, based upon such an idea, ought to be rejected at once, as tending to the public injury.

Still, however, as the project has been started, it may be well to inquire what is the greatest quantity of water that the present contents of the main spring can by any possibility supply to a single well. We have already seen that a slope of 10 feet per mile is not only sufficient to force the water through the earth, but also that it will force the water fast enough to carry off all the annual accessions to the main spring, whether from rain or any other cause.

Salt water will flow through the earth as easily as fresh water; and therefore, a head of 10 feet per mile will drive salt water through the earth; and, consequently, if a well is one mile from salt water, and is pumped down lower than 10 feet below the tide, the salt water will run down into the well and ruin it.

There is, therefore, an absolute limit to the *depth* to which a well can be pumped down and yield fresh water.

That limit is this: no well can be permanently drawn down more than 10 feet below tide for every mile of its distance from salt water.

The width of this end of the Island, from tide water to tide water, never exceeds 10 miles, the half of which is 5 miles.

A well in the centre of the Island, with a district to drain of 5 miles in every direction, could not be drawn down lower than 50 feet below tide. It would be impracticable to construct such a well; and moreover, there can be no doubt that a head of much less than 10 feet per mile would let the salt water enter in sufficient quantity to ruin the well.

Let it, however, be admitted that it is 50 feet below tide; that the top of the main spring is on an average 11 feet above tide; and that the area is a circle 10 miles in diameter.

This well will be able to exhaust a portion of the main spring 61 feet in depth, bounded on the top by a circle 10 miles in diameter, and on every side by lines reaching from the outer edge of this circle down to the bottom of the well. This drained portion of the main spring would be a conical or funnel shaped mass of saturated sand, 10 miles across at the top, 61 feet deep, running to a point at the bottom of the well, and shaped like an inverted cone or funnel.

The solid contents of this mass of saturated sand would be equal to 44,521 millions of cubic feet.

Sand can absorb about one third of its bulk of water; but it would be extremely difficult to pump out more than one quarter of its bulk of water; or in other words the quantity of available water in such a mass will not exceed one quarter of its bulk.

One quarter of the solid contents of that portion of the main spring which the well could exhaust, would amount to 11,130 millions of cubic feet. One cubic foot of water contains 6,232 imperial gallons; and therefore the total amount of water that could by any possibility be drawn from the present contents of the main spring by a single well, amounts to 69,364 millions of gallons. This, at 20 millions per day, would give a supply for nine years and a half.

The ultimate drainage area of this well would be 78 square miles.

That is to say: as the water of the main spring was exhausted, and the effective depth of the well increased by the depression of the water, the area of the drainage would gradually be extended to 78 square miles, every spring and well of which district would be ruined And as the same result would ensue from the adoption of any other plan which proposes to take more water than is annually introduced into the main spring, it appears to me to be clear, that every project must be rejected which proposes to rely upon any other source than the annual accessions of water to the main spring.

If the present contents of the main spring, within an area of 78 square miles, will only furnish a supply for less than ten years, and after a few years more the whole supply must be drawn from the water that is annually introduced into the main spring, the next step is to ascertain how much water is annually introduced, and how much of it we can appropriate to our own use. A circle of 78 square miles would be 10 miles in every direction; and it is very important to know how large a portion we shall be allowed to take, for our own exclusive use, of all the water provided by Providence for the wants of such a large district of country.

It appears to me to be impossible that we could be allowed to abstract more, at the very extreme, than one half of the annual supply.

In the case of an aqueduct, we do no injury to any part of the country above the line of the aqueduct, because we take what passes by them to us, and what they could not use—in fact we take the water second hand.

In the case of wells it would be very different:—as before shown, the water would run down to the wells on a slope, which slope is deeper and deeper beneath the main spring, as it approaches the well; and if the well is deep, the slope will be below the level of ordinary springs and wells, and will consequently dry them up; so that when we take the water by means of deep wells, we do not take it second hand; we absolutely turn it out of its appointed courses into new channels, for our own purposes, and to the very great injury of our neighbors.

Our investigations thus far have been upon the hypothesis that the substratum of the Island is, upon an average, as porous as between Fulton avenue and Flushing avenue, or between Franklin avenue (at Wyckoff street) and Gowanus.

This may be so or it may not. If the Island is not porous, then the water must run in veins:—such a supposition will render the well plan so very uncertain as to kill it. A large part of the main spring drains to the ocean through streams. This is clearly because that is the easiest way. The water has a certain head, which is just high enough to force it into the streams. If a lower head would force it through the earth to the ocean, then the main spring would fall down to that head, and drain that way. It is, then, certain that the slope of the streams is, at all events, not greater than what is necessary for subterranean drainage. By inspecting the table of streams, page 112, it will be seen that the slope of the streams varies from 6 to 9 feet per mile; and consequently that the assumed slope of 10 feet per mile cannot be much too large; and I do not think it would be at all safe to base any great work upon a less slope.

We have already seen that with a slope of 10 feet per mile we cannot drain deeper than 50 feet.

In my opinion it is highly probable that in practice another limit will be found to the depth of our wells, besides the one above stated.

It was for many years a rule in this city to sink the wells 5 feet below tide level.

Almost all of our old city wells give hard water;—and so do some of the wells in the country.

Generally speaking all the wells which draw their supply from near tide level, give hard water, provided they are fully used, so as to exhaust the water that has accumulated at a higher level.—Whether it is because marine remains exist at and below tide level, or that mineral water is heavier than soft water, or because the upper springs have been able to force out the impurities, I cannot say; but as a general fact I cannot doubt it.

There are some deep wells which give soft water; but in all of them the water rises above tide, showing that they have not yet exhausted the upper part of the main spring;—and several of them are sunk into veins, as is clearly shown by the fact that the water rose up and filled them almost instantly after the crust was pierced through.

The depth of a well, as before shown, limits the extent of its drainage area, and consequently the amount of its yield which will at the utmost be equal to all the water that is annually introduced into the area drained, whether by rain or from any other source.

According to the principle we have laid down, that we cannot be allowed to use more than one half of the water of the country, one single well, in order to effect the object proposed must drain a district or area capable of yielding at least twice the amount of water proposed to supply; and also do it in such a way that after our supply is drawn out, the remainder can be applied to the wants of the country.

Our next step, therefore, is to ascertain, as nearly as possible, the total quantity of water that is annually introduced into the main spring, or rather the total quantity that the main spring can furnish in dry seasons.

As before shown, the total amount of all the water which enters the main spring, year by year, is passed through it into the ocean—otherwise those wells that are upon low ground would run over. In addition to this, all the surface drainage of the conntry passes off through the streams to the ocean, which two quantities taken together make up the sum total of all the water discharged from the Island into the ocean, and this total can be very nearly ascertained. But it is a difficult matter to say what portion is due to surface drainage, and what portion to subterranean drainage. And as the wells cannot store up anything, they must, in dry seasons, depend entirely upon subterranean drainage.

In dry seasons there is little or no surface drainage, and at such times the streams must be supplied from springs, which are the outlets or discharging points of the subterranean drainage from the main spring to the ocean.

The quantity of water flowing in the streams at such times is a correct measure of the efflux from the main spring; and as it has been already shown that during the course of ages an equilibrium has been established between the influx and the efflux, that quantity must be equal to all the available water thrown into the main spring, from all sources whatever.

By an inspection of the table of streams, in Mr. McAlpine's Report, it will be seen that they ascend at from 6 to 9 feet per mile from tide, and that, consequently, at equal distances from tide they are at nearly equal elevations.

From this fact it is natural to suppose that the main spring, between any two streams, would drain both ways from a line about half way between the streams.

The general surface of the country is very level, nevertheless it is lower near the streams than midway between them: and as the slopes appear to have been formed by the action of flowing water, it is probable that, as a general fact, the ridges which divide the surface drainage are also midway between the streams, or that the area of the surface drainage into any stream is about equal to the area of the subterranean drainage into the same.

At all events, if we take a large extent of country the small difference that may exist in the two outside districts will form but a small per centage of the whole; and we can thus obtain a very close approximation to the truth. The surface drainage into Parsonage Creek is stated to be equal to 21 and 74-100 square miles. In October, 1852, Mr. Nash found the yield of the stream to be equal to 7,492,000 gallons per diem, or 344,618 gallons per day per square mile.

Again, it is stated that the whole drainage from Jamaica Creek to East Meadow Creek somewhat exceeds 100 square miles, and that it yields in dry seasons 32,250,000 gallons per day, which is equal to 322,500 gallons per day per square mile, which is the total amount of the available accessions to the main spring.

If we assume the larger ratio—that is, 344,618 gallons per day per square mile, as the true measure of all the available accessions to the main spring, then it will take 29-10 square miles of area to supply one million of gallons per day, year by year, provided we appropriate *all the water* in the country.

If we take only one half of the annual supply of the country, we require, at least, 116 square miles of area to furnish 20 millions per day.

As before stated, the drainage area of the largest well that can, by any possibility, be constructed on this end of the Island, is 78 square miles; and, therefore, it is impossible to derive our supply from any single well, even if it could be constructed. It is, therefore, not necessary to carry this part of the investigation farther.

The average level of the main spring is 11 feet above tide; and as it would not be either prudent or desirable to draw the wells down much below tide, the effective depths of the wells would average from 10 to 12 feet.

Such wells, with a head of 10 feet per mile, could be expected to drain one mile every way from the well. Their drainage area would average three square miles per well; and if we take the yield of the main spring to be equal to 344,618 gallons per mile per day, as was found to be the case at Parsonage Creek, such wells could furnish about one million of gallons per well per diem.

Whether powerful engines could be kept in good working order on sand bottoms is questionable.

The County House well is said to furnish 300,000 gallons per day.

Mr. Wood's well 144,000.

Mr. Wilson's well about 432,000.

The two last mentioned pumps have solid foundations. The old County House well was undermined and fell in.

I have been told that the new well has settled two feet, but not that the machinery has been deranged.

In order not to disparage the well project, let it be admitted that the wells can supply one million of gallons each. We should require 20 wells, distributed over an area of at least 116 square miles.

They could not be less than 2 1-2 miles apart. The length of the connecting conduits would exceed 50 miles. Their location would be so controlled by the location of the wells, as to preclude much choice of ground.

The excavation, would without a doubt, be very expensive.

The aggregate amount of water to be passed through these conduits is the same as that to be passed through the aqueduct, while their length is more than three times as great as the length of the aqueduct.

A trunk two feet square will pass four times as much water as a trunk one foot square, while it will cost less than three times as much; so that upon general principles this conduit ought to cost more than the aqueduct, which last can, moreover, be located upon the most favorable ground.

The wells, pumps, steam engines and buildings, will certainly swell the first cost, and afterwards be a perpetual source of trouble and expense.

The drainage district would extend out upon the Island further than the line of the aqueduct: and as all the ponds would be ruined by taking away half their water, they would have to be paid for in either case, while the land damages must be greatest on the longest line.

The main pump, the reservoirs, and the distributing, would be the same in both cases.

In the case of the aqueduct, the water would flow to the main pump naturally, by its own force.

In the case of the well system, it would have to be first pumped from the bowels of the earth.

The aqueduct is cheap, simple, and certain.

The well system is expensive and complicated, and in the very nature of things must be uncertain.

An aqueduct would be supplied from the sources above ground, which are subject to inspection, and capable of being measured with considerable accuracy.

Wells would depend upon subterranean sources, which are hidden from sight, and only susceptible, at best, of being estimated by probabilities.

Very Respectfully,
Your Obedient Servant,
JOHN S. STODDARD.

DOCUMENT, NO. TEN.

REPORT,

OF THE

WATER COMMITTEE,

SUBMITTED SEPTEMBER 18TH, 1854

WITH REPORT ON THE FLOW

OF THE

LONG ISLAND STREAMS.

REPORT.

The undersigned, to whom was referred the resolutions hereunto annexed, Report:

That in compliance with said resolutions, they obtained the valuable services of Messrs. Robert Leigh, George Stoddard and J. Carson Brevoort, for the purpose of ascertaining the quantity of water daily flowing from the ponds on the Island, from which it is proposed to obtain a supply of water for the city of Brooklyn. The result of the investigation is hereto annexed, which precludes the necessity of making an elaborate report upon the important subject which it involves.

A brief statement, however, may not be inappropriate, inasmuch as it has been frequently asserted that the supply from these sources in dry seasons would be inadequate to the present and increasing population of the city of Brooklyn.

By comparing the result of the investigation referred to, with the report submitted to the Common Council, March 13, 1854, it will be seen that it varies but little from the guagings made in October, 1852, the latter showing a small increase over the former.

When it is recollected that the present season has been the driest one we have had for many years, and the result of a scientific investigation shows an increase in the flow of water from these ponds, it is apprehended there can be but little doubt in the mind of any reasonable man as to the quanity of water obtainable from these ponds.

In addition to the quantity of the water as reported by the Engineers, the Committee from a personal inspection of the ponds, are of the opinion that the quality of the water during the late severe drought and hot weather, is as pure as in the most favorable season.

The undersigned are of the opinion now, as heretofore, that if the city of Brooklyn is ever supplied with water, it must be from the sources contemplated in the report formerly snbmitted, and upon the plan heretofore adopted by the Common Council. It may be, however, that the plan formerly adopted by the Common Council, and submitted to the people for their approval, may hereafter be changed in some slight and unimportant particular, with the view of satisfying the citizens of Brooklyn that the opposition was not wholly unfounded.

The undersigned are gratified to learn that those who were instrumental in misleading the citizens of Brooklyn upon a subject of vital importance to their best interests, are beginning to acknowledge their error, and admit that a sufficient supply can be had from the sources heretofore contemplated by the Common Council. Sophistry and misstatements may for awhile be substituted for reason, and the results of scientific investigations, but the community never fail to detect the error, and when detected, those who inflicted the wrong always receive their just condemnation.

The result of the investigation hereto annexed, is but an additional evidence of the accuracy of the former report, and shows that any further investigation upon that point would be a useless expenditure of money, and afford no additional light upon this all important question.

In the discharge of the duties devolved upon the undersigned, they have been governed by a desire to promote the best interests of Brooklyn; and they feel assured that their labors will hereafter be appreciated, and the plan they submitted for the supply of the city with water approved. All which is respectfully submitted.

Brooklyn, Sept. 18, 1854.

JOHN A. DAYTON,
R. C. BRAINARD,
F. G. QUEVEDO, } Water Committee.
D. P. BARNARD,
SAMUEL BOOTH.

Adopted, and ordered to be embodied in the papers on the subject, now printing, and also to be inserted three times in the Corporation papers.

September 18, 1854.

JOSEPH HEGEMAN, Clerk.

Approved September 20, 1854.

EDWARD A. LAMBERT, Mayor.

[COPY.]

In Common Council,
September 4th, 1854.

By ALDERMAN WILSON.

Resolved, That Messrs. Ludlum & Stoddard be, and are hereby directed to guage the principal streams on Long Island, from which the City expects to derive a supply of water.

Water Committee, with power, by unanimous consent.

By ALDERMAN DAYTON:

Resolved, That in case either of the persons named to guage the water streams shall not be able to attend, the Water Committee shall have power to substitute other suitable persons.

Adopted by unanimous consent.

JOSEPH HEGEMAN, Clerk.

Approved September 6, 1854.

EDWARD A. LAMBERT, Mayor.

To Messrs.

JOHN A. DAYTON,
R. C. BRAINARD,
D. P. BARNARD,
F. G. QUEVEDO,
SAMUEL BOOTH,

Water Committe of the Common Council of the City of Brooklyn.

GENTLEMEN:

Having been instructed to measure the quantity of water issuing from certain ponds on Long Island, in order to ascertain the effect of this unexampled duration of dry weather, we commenced operations, and were fortunately enabled to complete the work by Saturday, September 9th, and before the subsequent rainy weather had commenced.

Before giving the result of the guages, we may remark that the verification of those more elaborately made on former occasions, being the chief object in view, the occasion did not wrrrant the expense or inconvenience attendant upon drawing off the ponds, in order to obtain the natural flow of the streams, since nearly, if not quite, as accurate results were to be arrived at by calculating the water running from the mill at its usual rate and time. Thus at Baiseley's we found they worked regularly ten hours per day on the average, except on Sundays, when, however, it became necessary, owing to the excessive accumulation of water, to draw off the pond. By measuring then the flow as we found it, and taking ten (10) hours for a day, we make the yield 5,608,800 imperial gallons.

On the occasion of our visit the pond had a full head of water, minus one inch and a half which it had fallen during the previous six hours. We were informed that a few days ago the waste gate having been carried away, the pond was run dry, or rather reduced to the natural channel of the stream, but on the breach being repaired, the water acquired its ordinary height in forty-eight hours.

We may also here observe that in all the ponds there was the same full head of water, and the supply seemed to be scarcely, if at all, affected by this protracted drought.

At Nostrand's pond an estimate could not so satisfactorily be made, owing to the frequent stoppages in working the saw mill, but by guaging the flume and using the floats while the saw was going, and deducting one-fourth of the days work for said stoppages, making eight hours instead of ten, we could not possibly be much in error, and accordingly we make 2,905,358 gallons as the daily supply.

Simonsons' mill works eight hours on the average, and the pond falls about four inches in that time.

The dam of the upper pond having given way on the previous day, the water was not in a condition for accurate guaging. We offer the result, however, such as we found it—viz 2,083,800 gallons.

P. Cornwell's pond averages eight hours, and the supply is 3,508,659 gallons.

L. Cornwell's or Parsonage Creek has an abundance of water, and though assured the mill worked night and day last week, we prefer estimating at the ordinary days work of ten hours, by which we make 9,385,656 gallons.

As the amount we give is the result of many careful trials, we can guarantee its comparative accuracy, as far as we were concerned, and fully believing the average times taken as a days work, are correct, or by no means in excess, we are confident the supply, if anything, exceeds the quantity we make.

SYNOPSIS.

	Imperial Gallons per Day.
Baiseley's	5,608,800
Nostrand's	2,905,358
Simonson's	2,083,980
P. Cornwell's	3,508,659
L. Cornwell's or Parsonage Creek	9,385,656
Total	23,492,453

Very Respectfully,

Your obedient Servants,

ROBERT LEIGH,

GEORGE STODDARD,

J. CARSON BREVOORT.

Brooklyn, September 16, 1854.

DOCUMENT NO. ELEVEN.

AN ACT

TO

SUPPLY THE CITY OF BROOKLYN

WITH WATER,

PASSED JUNE 3RD, 1853,

WITH THE AMENDMENTS,

PASSED APRIL 7TH, 1854.

AN ACT.

FOR THE SUPPLY OF THE CITY OF BROOKLYN WITH WATER.

PASSED JUNE 3RD, 1853, THREE FIFTHS BEING PRESENT.

The People of the State of New York represented in Senate and Assembly, do enact as follows:

SEC. 1. The Common Council of the City of Brooklyn may determine, provisionally, from what sources and in what manner, the said city shall be supplied with water; but before such plan shall be executed, an intelligible outline of it, with the estimated cost of its execution, shall be published in the Corporation Papers for fifteen days, and the sense of the electors of said city, upon such plan, shall be taken as hereinafter provided.

SEC. 2. The Common Council shall cause a poll to be opened in each election district of said city, on or after the fifteenth day subsequent to the first publication of said plan, of which poll fifteen days notice shall be given in said Corporation Papers. The inspectors of election in the several election districts last elected, shall preside at such election, and any vacancies in the office of such inspectors shall be filled by the Common Council in the mode prescribed by law. The said electors shall express their approval or disapproval of said plan by each depositing in the ballot box, a ballot containing the words written or printed thereon, " in favor of the water plan," or " against the water plan," and such ballots shall be endorsed " water plan," and the election laws of this State, so far as applicable, shall apply to said election, except as herein otherwise provided. A canvass and return of said votes shall be made by the inspectors of election in the same manner as is prescribed by law in regard to the canvass and return of votes for charter officers, and the Common Council, at its next regular meeting thereafter, shall proceed to determine, and shall declare and publish, the result of such poll, and such determination and publication shall be conclusive evidence in all courts and places that such election was duly held, and of the result thereof.

SEC. 3. If a majority of such electors shall be declared to have voted in favor of the water plan, the Common Council and Commissioners shall proceed to execute such plan in the mode hereinafter prescribed. If a majority of such electors shall be declared to have voted against the water plan, the Common Council may proceed from time to time, in the mode herein above provided, to submit other plans and estimates to said electors, until the approval of a plan by said electors shall be obtained; and the plan so approved shall be carried into effect, as herein provided.

SEC. 4. After any plan submitted to the electors shall have been approved as herein provided, the Common Council, by a majority vote of all the members elected thereto, shall appoint five Commissioners, who shall be known as the "Water Commissioners of the City of Brooklyn," and shall hold their offices until the water works hereinafter mentioned are constructed and completed, and water distributed by them, unless their office should be sooner terminated, as hereinafter provided; but they, or either of them, may be removed for cause, by a vote of two-thirds of the members elected to the Common Council, after having had an opportunity to be heard in their defence; and any vacancy which may occur in said Board, from any cause whatever, shall be filled by the appointment of other commissioners by the Common Council, who shall hold office for the residue of said term. A majority of said commissioners shall be a quorum for the exercise of the powers and performance of the duties of said office.

SEC. 5. No commissioner shall receive any compensation, fee or perquisite, or be in any manner, directly or indirectly, interested in any contract for any property, work or materials connected with the works authorized by this act, under penalty of forfeiture of his office.

SEC. 6. The said commissioners may employ such counsel, and as many clerks, inspectors, superintendents, engineers and surveyors, and such subordinate assistants as may be necessary for the performance of the duties under this act, which the commissoners may prescribe.

SEC. 7. The said commissioners shall have power to make conditional contracts, subject to ratification by the said Common Council, with the owner or owners of all lands, tenements, hereditaments, rights and privileges whatsoever, which may be required for said works, for the purchase thereof, at stated prices, which contracts shall be so drawn as to be binding upon such owners, in case the same shall be ratified by the Common Council within one year from the date thereof; and also to make all other contracts, for the work and materials required for the construction and completion of said works, subject in like manner, to ratification by the Common Council.

SEC. 8. All contracts for work to be done, or materials to be used, in the construction of the said works, shall be made in writing, and of each contract there shall be at least three copies, which shall be numbered with the same number, and endorsed with the date of the contract, the name of the contractor, and a summary of the work to be done, or materials furnished. One of said copies shall be retained by the commissioners, and another shall be deposited with the comptroller of the city.

SEC. 9. Public notice shall be given of the time and place at which sealed proposals will be received for entering into contracts. All such proposals for contracts shall be for a sum certain as to the price to be paid or received, and no proposition which is not thus definite or certain, or which contains any alternative condition or limitation, as to price, or the security hereinafter mentioned, be given, shall be received or acted on.

SEC. 10. No more than one proposition shall be received from any one person for the same contract, and all the propositions of the person who shall, directly or indirectly, offer or be in any way interested in more than one proposition, shall be rejected. All bids and proposals for any contract shall be filed in the office of the City Clerk, within ten days after such contract shall have been signed, and the security given as hereinafter provided.

Sec. 11. Every person who shall enter into any contract for the supply of materials, or the performance of labor, shall give satisfactory security to the commissioners for the faithful performance of his contract, according to its terms.

Sec. 12. All materials procured or contracted for, to be used in the construction of said works, shall be exempt from execution; but the Common Council shall pay the money due for such materials to the judgment creditors of the contractor or their assigns, out of any monies due upon such contract, from the City of Brooklyn, at the time of the receipt of a written notice of such execution, and under which execution such materials might otherwise have been sold, upon production to them of due proof that such execution would have attached; and such payment shall be held a valid payment on the contract and on the judgment.

Sec. 13. Every voluntary assignment of any contract made with the said commissioners for labor or materials to be employed upon said works, shall be absolutely void, unless ratified by the Common Council, and shall also subject such contract to forfeiture, at the option of the Common Council.

Sec. 14. The Common Council shall authorise the commissioners, with the sanction of the Mayor, the Chairman of the Water Committee, and the Chairman of the Finance Committee of said Common Council, or any two of them, to draw upon the comptroller of the city for any sum in favor of, and to be paid to the owner of any lands, waters, streams, water rights and privileges, or other property acquired by virtue of this act, and in favor of, and to be paid to any contractor for any sum due upon his contract, and also for any other expenses incurred by them, under section six of this act. Such drafts shall specify the objects for which they are drawn, as nearly as may be; and the Common Council shall make it the duty of the comptroller to pay such drafts, with said sanction, in every case where a deed or other voucher is delivered to him, or a copy of a contract has been filed in his office; and a duplicate receipt of the contractor for such draft shall be presented therewith.

Sec. 15. The comptroller shall, once in each month, report to the Common Council a list of all the payments made by him upon the drafts of the commissioners; and previous to such monthly report the accounts of the commissioners and of the comptroller, in respect of such payments, shall be examined by the Water and Finance Committees of the Common Council.

Sec. 16. The commissioners shall report to the said Common Council, quarterly, and at all other times when required by them, a general exhibition of the state of the works, including a full detail of the amount expended, and of the progress made in the construction.

Sec. 17. The said Common Council may, in the manner hereinafter provided, take any lands, tenements, hereditaments, rights and privileges whatsoever, which may be required by said works, in pursuance of such plan as they shall adopt; and may use the ground or soil under any street, turnpike or railroad, or other road, or highway within this State, for the purpose of introducing water into said city, on condition that they shall cause the surface of the street, highway or road to be restored to its original state, and all damages done thereto to be repaired; and in general may do any other act or thing necessary or convenient and proper for effecting the purpose of this act.

Sec. 18. The said commissioners and their agents, are hereby authorised to enter upon any land or water for the purpose of making surveys, and to agree with the owner of any property which may be required for the purposes of this act, as to the amount of compensation to be paid to such owner; but no contract for real estate or water rights shall be valid and binding, until the same shall have been ratified by the Common Council.

Sec. 19. The said Common Council shall be liable to pay all damages that may be sustained by any persons or corporation in their property, by the taking of any land, water, or water rights, or by the constructing of any aqueducts, reservoirs, or other works for the purposes of this act. And if the owner of any land, water, or water rights, which shall be required for the purposes aforesaid, or any other person who shall sustain damage as aforesaid, shall not agree with the said commissioners upon the damages or compensation to be paid therefor, or in case such owner or person shall be an infant, a married woman, or insane, or shall be absent from this State, application may be made in the premises by the said Water Commissioners, to one of the Justices of the Supreme Court, at any special term thereof, held in the County of Kings, or in the City of New York, upon a notice of ten days, served upon the other party or parties. Upon such application, the said justice shall appoint three judicious and disinterested citizens of this State, as Commissioners of Estimate, who shall, after reasonable notice to all the parties, take testimony if offered, examine such property, estimate the value thereof, or the damage sustained thereby, and make a report thereon without delay. Upon completing such report, they shall file the same in the Office of the County of Kings, where it shall be open to the inspection of all parties interested therein; and the said Commissioners of Estimate shall give notice to all the parties of the completion and filing of said report.

Sec. 20. After said report shall have been so filed, either party may, upon a notice of not less than twenty days, to all the other parties interested therein, present the said report to the Supreme Court, at any special term thereof, for confirmation. Any party or parties may, within twenty days after receiving such notice, appeal from the said report, by serving a notice thereof upon the other party or parties, at least ten days before the time at which the said report is to be presented to said court for confirmation; which notice shall be accompanied by copies of any affidavits which have been presented to said Commissioners of Estimate, and which the appellant shall intend to use on such appeal; and also with a brief statement in writing, of the grounds of objection to such report, and of the manner in which it is contended that the same ought to be altered. Such appeal shall be heard when the said report shall be presented to the court for confirmation. No affidavits shall be read against confirming said report, except those of which copies shall have been served as aforesaid; but affidavits may be read in support of said report. Upon such hearing, the court may confirm such report, or may send it back to the same, or other commissioners, for a further or new report. Such new report shall be made, filed, presented for confirmation, and appealed from, in all respects as above provided; and as often as any such report shall be referred, the like proceeding shall be thereupon had. In any case, however, where the court can and shall direct specific alterations to be made therein, and such alterations shall be made during the same term, the said report may be thereupon absolutely confirmed. Such report, when confirmed, shall be conclusive upon all parties. If neither party shall notice the said report for confirmation, within thirty days after notice shall have been given of its filing as aforesaid, the same shall be null and void; and the said Water Commissioners may apply for the appointment of new Commissioners of Estimate, as hereinbefore provided, who shall proceed in the same manner as if no others had been appointed.

Sec. 21. All costs of said proceedings shall be paid by the said Water Commissioners, except where an appeal is taken, in which case the court shall have power to award costs against the appellant, in cases where the appeal shall not be prosecuted or sustained. All costs and reasonable counsel fees in such proceedings, and in the construction of said water works, and generally in the execution of this act, shall be taxed and certified by the County Judge of Kings County, or one of the Justices of the Supreme Court, and be paid by the comptroller to the parties and persons on whose behalf such costs and fees have been taxed, upon presentation of the taxed bill or bills. After such report shall have been confirmed, the said Water Commissioners shall, within three months thereafter, pay or tender to such owner, or to such person or persons as the court may direct, the sum mentioned in such report, in full compensation for the property so required, or for the damages sustained; and thereupon, the City of Brooklyn shall become seized in fee of such property so required, and shall be discharged from all claim by reason of such damages. All parties having liens upon such premises may be made parties to the above proceedings, and the amounts payable to each shall be designated in said report.

Sec. 22. In all cases where personal notice cannot be served, pursuant to the preceding sections of this act, by reason of the absence of any party or parties, it shall be sufficient to publish such notice directed to such party or parties by name, for the number of days which such notice is herein required to be given, in each of the Corporation Newspapers of the City of Brooklyn. The said court shall, on the application of any party, appoint guardians ad libitem, to protect the interests of parties under legal incapacity; and thereupon, such parties shall be in all respects concluded by the proceedings to the same extent as if they could have, and had, personally appeared.

Sec. 23. The Common Council may, by a vote of two-thirds of the members elected thereto, close and strike from the city map, such streets and avenues, and such parts of streets and avenues as may be required in the construction, equipment and operation of said water works.

Sec. 24. For the purpose of paying the cost of said water works, together with all incidental expenses and damages, the said Common Council are hereby authorised to raise by loan, from time to time, in such amounts as they may deem expedient, a sum sufficient to complete and finish the same, by the issue of bonds or the creation of a public debt or stock, to be called "The Water Stock of the City of Brooklyn," which shall bear an interest not exceeding six per cent. per annum, payable semi-annually, and shall be payable or redeemable at a period of time not less than fifteen nor more than forty years from and after the passage of this act. Such bonds or stock may be sold by the Common Council at public or private sale, at not less than the nominal or par value thereof.

SEC. 25. In addition to the sums of money authorized to be procured by loan under the preceding section of this act, the Common Council, may, whenever and so far as may be necessary, issue and dispose of other bonds or stocks, in the manner prescribed in said section, as part of said water stock, to meet all payments of interest which may accrue upon any bonds or stock by them issued under said section; provided, however, that no bond or scrip shall be issued for the payment of interest as aforesaid, after the expiration of one year from the completion of said works; but the payment of all interest that shall accrue after that time, shall be made as hereinafter provided.

SEC. 26. All moneys to be raised by virtue of this act, whether by loan or by tax, shall be exclusively expended and applied to and for the purposes specified herein, under the direction of the said Commissioners, or as herein otherwise provided, and shall be appropriated or devoted to no other use or purpose whatever.

SEC. 27. The Common Council shall, from time to time regulate the price or rents for the use of water to be supplied through said works, so as to pay from the net income to be derived from said works, the semi-annual interest upon, and ultimately the principal of, said bonds or stocks, so far as the same may be practicable and reasonable. And after payment or deduction of all expenses and charges of distribution, the net surplus income from said water works shall be set apart as a sinking fund, and shall be appropriated for and towards the payment of the principal and interest of the said water stock, and shall be under the management, control and direction of the Mayor, treasurer and comptroller of the said city, or the major part of them for the time being, who shall be Commissioners of the said fund, to be applied solely to the use and purpose aforesaid, until the principal and interest of the said water stock shall be fully paid and discharged.

SEC. 28. The Common Council shall make timely and ample provision for the redemption of said bonds or stock, principal and interest; to that end they shall ascertain and determine from time to time what sum will be required to be paid annually to meet the semi-annual accruing interest not herein otherwise provided for, and also to provide for the payment of the principal of said water stock when the same shall become payable; and if it shall appear in any year after the said works shall be put in operation, and the water distributed thereby, that the net surplus income mentioned in the preceding section of this act, shall not amount to the sum so ascertained and determined to be the proportion which shall be paid in such year, such actual or anticipated deficiency shall be levied and collected by tax in the same manner as is now provided by law for levying and collecting the taxes for the support of said city, and as a part of the next annual taxes of said city.

SEC. 29. The moneys directed by this act to be paid into the sinking fund, shall be invested by the Commissioners of said sinking fund in the several and respective public stocks or bonds, issued by the City of Brooklyn, by the County of Kings, by the State of New York and by the United States.

SEC. 30. The Common Council may organize a department with full powers for the management of said works and the distribution of the said water; and may also pass by-laws and ordinances for the regulation, protection and preservation of the said works, provided that such by-laws and ordinances shall not be inconsistent with any law of this State, and shall be subject to be modified or repealed by the Legislature.

SEC. 31. If any person shall wilfully do, or cause to be done, any act whereby any work, materials or property whatsoever, erected or used or hereafter to be erected or used within said city, or elsewhere by the Commissioners or Common Council, or by any person acting under their authority, for the purpose of procuring or keeping a supply of water, shall in any manner be injured, or shall corrupt said water or render it impure, every such person or persons shall forfeit and pay to said city three times the amount of the damages that shall be assessed therefor, to be recovered by the Common Council in any proper action, and every such person shall be deemed guilty of a misdemeanor, and be indictable and punishable therefor.

SEC. 32. Nothing in this contained shall authorize the taking of water from the Croton river or the Croton aqueduct, without the consent of the Mayor, Aldermen and Commonalty of the City of New York.

SEC. 33. The Common Council may agree with the corporate authorities of the City of Williamsburgh, to supply that city with water upon the same terms and conditions as are paid by the citizens of Brooklyn.

SEC. 34. Nothing in this act contained shall be so construed as to interfere with the rights, privileges and immunities now held by the corporation, created by the act entitled "An Act to Incorporate the Williamsburgh Water Works Company," passed April 16th, 1852. But it shall be lawful for the City of Brooklyn with the consent of a majority of the Board of Directors of the said corporation, and not otherwise, at any time hereafter, to take or purchase all the interest, property and effects of the said corporation at such price, and upon such terms as may be agreed upon by the Common Council of the said City of Brooklyn, and the said Williamsburgh Water Works Company; and the said Williamsburgh Water Works Company are hereby authorized to convey by deed, or otherwise, to the City of Brooklyn all their property, effects, rights, privileges and immunities, and upon the same being so conveyed, all the property rights, privileges and immunities of the said Williamsburgh Water Works Company, granted to them by their act of incorporation or any amendments thereof, or acquired under the same, shall absolutely vest in the said City of Brooklyn.

SEC. 35. So much of sections 26, 27 and 28 of the act entitled "An act to revise and Amend the Several Acts relating to the City of Brooklyn," passed April 4, 1850, passed June 19, 1851, as is inconsistent with the provisions of this act, are hereby repealed. But nothing herein contained shall be so construed as to impair any act done, contract made, or rights acquired by or on behalf of the said City of Brooklyn by virtue thereof; and all such acts, contracts and rights, are hereby confirmed.

SEC. 36. This act shall take effect immediately.

STATE OF NEW YORK,
SECRETARY'S OFFICE

I have compared the preceeding with the original law on file in this office, and hereby certify the same to be a correct transcript therefrom and of the whole of said original.

[L.S.] Given under my hand and seal of this office, at the city of Albany, this fourth day of June, one thousand eight hundred and fifty-three.

ARCHIBALD CAMPBELL, Dep. Secretary of State.

AMENDMENTS

TO THE ACT OF JUNE 3RD, 1853,—PASSED APRIL, 7TH, 1853.

The sections amended are to read as follows, the amendments being in italics:

SEC. 1   The Common Council of the City of Brooklyn may determine, provisionally, from what sources and in what manner, the said city shall be supplied with water, *amd whether by contract or otherwise;* but before such plan shall be executed, an intelligible outline of it, with the estimated cost of its execution, shall be published in the Corporation Papers for fifteen days, and the sense of the electors of said city, upon such plan, shall be taken as hereinafter provided.

SEC. 4.   After any plan submitted to the electors shall have been approved as herein provided, the Common Council, by a vote of *two-thirds* of all the members elected thereto, shall appoint *six* commissioners, who shall be known as the "Water Commissioners of the City of Brooklyn," and shall hold their offices until the water works hereinafter mentioned are constructed and completed, and water distributed by them, unless their office should be sooner terminated, as hereinafter provided; but they or either of them may be removed for cause, by a vote of two-thirds of the members elected to the Common Council, after having had an opportunity to be heard in their defence; and any vacancy which may occur in said Board, from any cause whatever, shall be filled by the appointment of other commissioners *by a vote of two thirds of all the members elected* to the Common Council, who shall hold office for the residue of said term.   A majority of said commissioners shall be a quorum for the exercise of the powers and performance of the duties of said office.

SEC. 24.   For the purpose of paying the cost of said water works, together with all incidental expenses and damages, the said Common Council are hereby authorized to raise by loan, from time to time, in such amounts as they may deem expedient, a sum *not exceeding four and a half millions of dollars;* by the issue of bonds or the creation of a public debt or stock, to be called "The Water Stock of the City of Brooklyn," which shall bear an interest not exceeding six per cent. per annum, payable semi-annually, and shall be payable or redeemable at a period of time not less than fifteen nor more than forty years from and after the passage of this act.   Such bonds or stock may be sold by the Common Council at public or private sale, at not less than the nominal or par value thereof.

DOCUMENT NO. TWELVE.

OUTLINE

OF

PLAN FOR SUPPLYING

THE

CITY OF BROOKLYN WITH WATER;

SUBMITTED TO THE ELECTORS,

JULY 11th, 1853.

The Common Council of the City of Brooklyn, in pursuance of an Act of the Legislature, entitled, "An act for the supply of the City of Brooklyn with Water, passed 3d June, 1853", have provisionally adopted a plan for such supply, of which the following is an outline:—

The sources from which the Water will be obtained, are East Meadow Brook, in the town of Hempstead; Parsonage Creek, also in said town, and intermediate streams, which have been or may be hereafter purchased for said purpose, and which are estimated to furnish water sufficient for the supply of a population four times as great as that contained in the City of Brooklyn, at the present time.

The analysis of the water which has been made, shows it to be purer than that supplied to any other city in the country, Boston only excepted.

P

Suitable dams or reservoirs will be constructed on said streams, and the water will be brought thence in a conduit, or partly in a conduit and partly in an open canal, at or near to the base of the line of hills forming the backbone of the Island, where the pump-well will be located, and the necessary steam engines and machinery erected to elevate the water to a reservoir to be located upon the summit of said line of hills, which reservoir will be of ample capacity to contain a supply beyond the daily wants of the city—and from thence the water will be distributed by iron pipes throughout the city, as the wants of the citizens, and the location of the population may require.

The conduit or canal will be constructed of suitable capacity to carry water sufficient, for at least four times our present population.

The estimated cost of bringing from the farthest point named, a sufficient supply of water for the present wants of the city, including the cost of streams, land, damages, conduit, pump well, steam engine and machinery, reservoirs and eighty miles of distribution pipes, hydrants, and all other things necessary to complete the work in the best manner, is four millions of dollars.

The additional cost, as the population of the city increases, will consist of such further steam power as might be necessary to elevate the additional quantity of water which might be required, and of such further distribution pipes as would be necessary to furnish the same to the consumers.

It is estimated that the cost of supplying a population double our present numbers, will, when required, add to the original cost of the work, one and a half millions of dollars.

DOCUMENT, NO. THIRTEEN.

REPORT OF PROGRESS

ON THE

WATER QUESTION,

SUBMITTED BY THE

WATER COMMITTEE

TO THE

COMMON COUNCIL

OF THE

CITY OF BROOKLYN.

DECEMBER, 1854.

[COPY.]

In Common Council, December, 7th 1854.

Resolved.—That the Water Committee be and are hereby authorised to print, in connection with the documents now being printed, by an order of this Common Council, a synopsis of the progress of the Water question, showing the various steps taken to the close of the year 1854, and have the same bound. Adopted by unanimous consent.

JOSEPH HEGEMAN, Clerk.

Approved December 11th, 1854.

EDWARD A. LAMBERT, Mayor.

To the Honorable the Common Council of the City of Brooklyn :

The Water Committe appointed by this Board, in the month of January last, herewith submit their annual report of progress on the Water Question, with such allusions to former progress and explanatory remarks, as the occasion requires.

Respectfully submitted,

JOHN A. DAYTON,
R. C. BRAINARD,
D. P. BARNARD,
E. G. QUEVEDO,
SAMUEL BOOTH.

Water Committee.

Brooklyn, December, 1854.

REPORT.

Your Committee, immediately after their appointment, fully impressed with the great importance of the interests committed to their charge, proceeded to avail themselves of the information previously obtained by former Committees on this question.

In examining the records, they found that, in the year 1847, some attention was paid to the sources of a supply, by a Special Committee, consisting of Aldermen D. A. Bokee, John Stanbury, and J. W. Cochran, who submitted, in the month of December, a brief Report, enclosing a letter from the late and deservedly celebrated civil engineer, Major D. B. Douglass, embodying his opinion as to the quantity of supply which might be obtained from the waters of Long Island. No professional examination further than this, seems to have been made at the time.

In 1848, Alderman George B. Fisk, Arthur W. Benson, William McDonald and J. W. Cochran were appointed a Special Committee on this subject, and a brief report of progress was made by them in January, 1849.

In December, 1851, Aldermen Charles R. Marvin, J. H. Smith, Edward Pell, Henry A. Kent, and E. B. Litchfield, Special Committee of the Common Council on this subject, submitted a Report, with communications from John B. Jervis and William J. McAlpine, Esquires, civil engineers of eminence, on the feasibility and adequacy of a supply from the Island sources.

This Report was preliminary to that published in December, 1852, by Aldermen Charles R. Marvin, Abraham B. Baylis, Montgomery Queen, George W. Stilwell, and Lemuel B. Hawxhurst, Standing Committee for that year, containing the Report in full of William J. McAlpine, Esq., who was employed by them to complete the examinations alluded to in the report of the previous year.

In debate of the Common Council, January 21, 1853, allusion to this question, in connection with the preliminary report, is thus made:

"Alderman Marvin commenced by giving a succinct history of the water project, and said, when the subject of obtaining a supply was first under consideration, a plan was submitted by Mr. Disbro, which was to sink wells in the neighborhood of Flatbush, and pump the water to a receiving reservoir, situated on Prospect Hill, by means of steam power, distributing it thence to the City. Upon inquiry and investigation, it was found that a sufficient quantity of water could not be obtained without a very great expense; that the works might not be of a character suited for manufacturing and domestic purposes, for which reason, among others, the proposition was declined. The next movement to this end, was commenced upon a report of Mr. McAlpine, the State Surveyor, who made an examination of the streams on Long Island, and advised that a supply be sought from this quarter. The report being preliminary only, was not considered by our citizens as sufficiently minute in its statements to warrant us in taking measures at that time to prosecute the enterprise, and a very general desire being expressed that the detailed estimates should be presented, the submission of the question informally to the people, which had been proposed, was postponed, and the Engineer was requested to perfect his plan and present the details of the cost. Measures have also been taken to guage the streams accurately and regularly since July last, and until nearly the close of the year. Those examinations have been satisfactory to the Committee, and the result is presented with the appendix to the report of the Engineer, Mr. McAlpine, That report was presented to the Common Council, and it was an able document, bearing upon it the evidence of care in its preparation, and it laid down a plan for obtaining a supply of water, which met the concurrence of the Water Committee, and of the late Board, and satisfied them that a supply of water was to be obtained from the Long Island streams."

In the report of Mr. McAlpine, the several sources of supply from the Croton River, from the Bronx River, and from wells in the vicinity of Brooklyn, are discussed, and it is shown conclusively that these cannot be depended on for the present and prospective use of this city.

The source of supply recommended, is found in the streams which enter the ocean on the southern side of the Island, commencing with Jamaica Creek, and ending with East Meadow Creek—the first being 13 miles from the Fulton Ferry, and 9 2-10th miles from the Pump well in the vicinity of Prospect Hill, and the last 25 miles from Fulton Ferry, and 21 3-10th miles from the Pump well. The quantity of supply from each stream, which might be taken, is thus stated:

NAME.	DISTANCE FROM PUMP WELL. Miles.	DAILY SUPPLY. Gallons.	AGGREGATE SUPPLY. Gallons.
Jamaica Creek	9.2	5,000,000	
Springfield " West Branch	11.0	1,500,000	6,500,000
" " East "	12.1	250,000	6,750,000
Hook " West "	12.2	4,000,000	10,750,000
" " Middle "	—	500,000	11,250,000
" " East "	14.2	2,000,000	13,250,000
Pine's "	16.2	2,000,000	15,250,000
Parsonage "	16.7	10,000,000	25,250,000
Millbrund "	19	2,000,000	27,250,000
East Meadow Creek	21.3	5,000,000	32.250,000

The general plan proposed, was to collect the water in reservoirs, "formed by raising the water in the streams by low dams to an elevation of from 12 to 25 feet above tide." From these reservoirs lateral conduits were to connect with a line of main aqueduct, which terminated at the Pump well located at Flatbush; thence the supply was to be "forced by steam engines and pumps through large iron mains, into the Distributing Reservoir on Prospect Hill, and thus distributed through the City by cast-iron pipes, in the usual manner.

The Estimates are adapted to five distinct plans of supply, which may be described as follows:

The First Plan is arranged for a present supply of five million gallons daily; providing for an extension to ten million gallons. The present supply is to be taken from Jamaica Creek, at Baiseley's Pond, by constructing a dam to raise the surface level from its present elevation of eight and one half feet above mean tide to thirteen and a half feet. The water to be conveyed to the Flatbush Pump Well by a brick aqueduct of oviform sections, with interior diameters of five and six feet, laid on a grade of six inches per mile, with a capacity for passing ten million gallons. To obtain ten million gallons supply, the aqueduct is extended easterly to Hook Creek, West Branch, with interior diameters of three and four feet. A dam and reservoir are constructed on Springfield Creek and on the West Branch of Hook Creek; provision is also made for a Storing Reservoir. The level of the water in P. Nostrand's Pond, (Springfield Creek) will be twenty-two and a quarter feet above tide; in the Reservoir on Hook Creek 16 feet above tide, and in the Storing Reservoir twenty-two feet above tide.

The estimated cost for the maximum supply is for

Distribution	$1,500,000.	
Distributing Reservoir	315,780.	
Engine House, &c.	631,500.	
Aqueducts, &c.	957,577.	
Contingencies, &c.	340,484.	$3,745,341.

The Second Plan is arranged for a present supply of five million gallons daily, providing for an extension to twenty million gallons. The present supply is to be taken from Jamaica Creek, as in the first plan: the aqueduct for the maximum supply being extended to Parsonage Creek. From the pump well to Jamaica Creek it is to be built of brick with plank and concrete foundations, with a semi-elliptical section, having interior diameters of eight and twelve feet, and a capacity of twenty millions of gallons:—thence to West Branch of Hook Creek, its capacity is reduced to fifteen million gallon; and thence to Parsonage Creek it has an oviform section with interior diameters of five and six feet. Its grade is six inches per mile. In addition to the dams and reservoirs of the First Plan, a dam is constructed at P. Cornwell's Pond (East Branch Hook Creek) raising it one foot above its present level, at Pine's Creek (or Pond) raising it five and a half feet, and at L. Cornwell's Pond, (Parsonage Creek) raising it four feet, or to a level of fourteen feet above tide. The height of the last pond is somewhat increased in addition for use as a Storing Reservoir.

The estimated cost for the maximum supply is for

Distribution	$2,000,000.	
Distributing Reservoir	315,780.	
Engine House, &c.	901,500.	
Aqueduct, &c.	1,781,823.	
Contingencies, &c.	499,910.	$5,499,013.

The Third Plan is arranged for a present supply of five million gallons daily, providing for an extension to thirty million gallons. The present supply is to be taken from Jamaica Creek, as in the First plan; the aqueduct for the maximum supply being extended to East Meadow Creek. From the pump well to Jamica Creek, its size is increased above the Second Plan to interior diameters of eleven and fourteen feet, and a capacity of thirty million gallons. Thence to Hook Creek, West Branch, its capacity is twenty-five million gallons; thence to Parsonage Creek, its interior diameters are eight and twelve feet; and thence to East Meadow Creek its section is oviform, with interior diameters of five and six feet, the grade being six inches per mile.

In addition to the dams and reservoirs of the Second Plan, a dam is constructed at Smart's Pond, which is the termination of the aqueduct. As its present surface level is eighteen feet above tide, and somewhat higher than requisite, its height is not increased.

The estimated cost for the maximum supply is for

Distribution	$2,500,000.	
Distributing Reservoir	315,780.	
Engine House, &c.	1,261,500.	
Aqueducts, &c.	2,711,170.	
Contingences, &c.	678,845.	$7,467,295.

The Fourth Plan is arranged for a present supply of five million gallons daily, providing for an extension to twenty millions. The present supply is to be taken from a reservoir constructed near the Jamaica dam, the bottom of which is twenty feet above tide, which is supplied through cast iron mains, by steam pumping machinery, erected at the mouth of Springfield Creek, 13,200 feet distant, The aqueduct from the Flatbush pump well to this reservoir is of brick, with five and a half and six and a half feet interior diameter, built on a grade of one foot per mile. The water from Jamaica creek will be conveyed easterly to the pump well at Springfield creek, by an aqueduct of three and four feet interior diameters, sloping one foot per mile. For the maximum supply, the water of Springfield creek will be taken into the pump well; the water of Parsonage creek will be conveyed to the West Branch of Hook Creek by an aqueduct of three and four feet interior diameters, and thence to the pump well the diameters are increased to five and a half and six and a half feet, the grade being six inches per mile.

The arrangement of the dams and reservoirs, is similar to that of the Second Plan.

The estimated cost for the maximum supply is, for

Distribution,	$2,000,000
Distributing Reservoir,	315,780
Engine House, &c., Flatbush,	894,500
" " Springfield Creek,	417,000
Aqueducts, &c.,	1,737,667
Contingencies, &c.,	536,494 $5,901,441

The Fifth plan is arranged for a present supply of five million gallons daily, providing for an extension to thirty million gallons. Its general arrangement is similar to that of the Fourth Plan.

The aqueduct from the reservoir near Baiseley's Pond to the Flatbush pump well, is increased to interior diameters of six and a half and eight feet. From East Meadow Creek to Parsonage Creek it is oviform, with interior diameters of five and six feet, on a grade of six inches per mile; thence to Hook Creek and the pump well, its section is semi-elliptical with interior diameters of eight and twelve feet. The dams and reservoirs are as in the Third Plan.

The estimated cost of the maximum supply is, for

Distribution,	$2,500,000
Distributing Reservoir,	315,780
Engine House, &c., Flatbush,	1,254,500
" " Springfield Creek,	542,000
Aqueducts, &c.,	2,516,235
Contingencies, &c.,	712,852 $7,841,367

The several estimates of cost above mentioned, are exclusive of the capital which represents the annual expense of pumping, &c.

The Report does not state which of the above plans is recommended for adoption. By reference to the outline of plan submitted to the people July 11, 1853, published herewith as Document No. Twelve, it will be observed that the plan therein contained, differs essentially in arrangement and cost from either of the above.

On the 80th page of this report, an Estimate of Distribution is given "for obtaining a supply of five million of gallons per day," embracing

30.22 miles pipe 4 inches diameter, with 50 stop cocks.
30.64 " 6 " " 50 "
38.89 " 8 " " 70 "
6.26 " 10 " " 10 "
12.60 " 12 " " 20 "
.74 " 16 ' " 5 "
.54 " 30 " " 1 "
1.60 " 36 " " 2 "
121.49 " in all.
1,000 Hydrants.

On pages 104 to 110, the arrangement of these pipes is given in an extended schedule. The estimate of cost is $1,289,200.

In the text following this estimate it is stated that "For the present population of the city, 80 miles of pipes would be a liberal provision, which would cost $900,000: which will be the estimate for the minimum supply on all the plans." The amounts estimated on pages 63 to 66 for distribution are, for

    The First Plan, Ten millions supply, . . . $1,500,000
    " Second " Twenty " . . . 2,000,000
    " Third " Thirty " . . . 2,500,000

It is evident, therefore, from these amounts, that the Schedule of Distribution above mentioned, is not adapted to either of the plans proposed.

The Distributing Reservoir estimated for in this Report is located on the summit of Prospect Hill. Its form is elliptical with the greatest diameters—viz: at the top of the embankments, six hundred and seventy-five, and nine hundred and thirty feet. Its surface elevation is one hundred and ninety feet above tide; its depth twenty feet; its surface area ten and one-third acres, and its contents about sixty million gallons. A division wall seperates it into two apartments.

For the first plan this Reservoir contains a supply for six days; for the second, a supply for three days; and for the third, a supply for two days. From the statement that it is located on the highest ground, and the omission of estimates for its extension, it is presumed that this capacity is all that can be advantageously obtained. In a note to page 28 on this subject, it is stated that "The plan of elevating the whole supply for the city into the Prospect Hill reservoir, may be modified by constructing another reservoir at an elevation of about one, hundred feet above tide, which would supply one half of the present population." No further mention of this secondary reservoir is made in the description of the pumping machinery, or in the estimates.

The style of pumping engine proposed in this Report, is a double-acting side lever, driving two plunger pumps from the side levers, and has a cylinder of seventy-two inches diameter, and twelve feet stroke. Its capacity is estimated at five million gallons, raised one hundred and ninety feet, working twelve hours, its maximum capacity for a longer working period being seven and one-half million gallons. For a supply of ten million gallons, an engine is proposed, with a cylinder of ninety-three inches diameter, and fifteen feet stroke, also double-acting. In the plans submitted with this report, elaborate drawings are made of the style of engine above described, but it is stated on page 49 that "the engine has been represented with side levers instead of a working beam, and the fly-wheel shaft has been placed on top of the engine frame. I have proposed to modify this plan in both respects; but as these changes will not increase the expense of the work, it is not regarded as important at the present time to make the correction."

An examination of the Report in question, of which a brief synopsis is thus given, made it evident to your Committee that it could not be taken as a guide, either as to the schedule of distribution, the location or locations of distributing reservoirs, the character of the pumping machinery, or the plan of the aqueducts and reservoirs, and they have felt impelled to mention this by the course of those who have made this Report, the chief argument against the conclusions subsequently presented, and not from any desire to affect in any way the established reputation of its author. They take this occasion to say, that aside from the points mentioned, it contains a large amount of statistical information, which they have found of very great service.

From the investigation of the former progress on this question, and on account of the reasons mentioned in our report of March 13th, Document No. One, your Committee were satisfied that it was necessary to make a new and thorough examination of this matter, with the best professional aid at their command. Under the authority of the Common Council they availed themselves of the services of Gen. Ward B. Burnett, U. S. Civil Engineer, in examining the work previously done, as well as such new suggestions as circumstances presented. The services of this gentleman were obtained not only from his position as an Engineer, but from the fact of his long connection with investigations similar to those the Committee were anxious to make.

As soon as it was determined to make a survey of the line of work, and to prepare plans and specifications, Samuel McElroy Esq. was requested to act as Principal Assistant to Gen. Burnett in their completion. This gentleman's experience on several of the prominent water works, canals, and other public works of this country, and as an officer of the Naval and Civil Engineer Corps of the United States, made his services valuable ; and with regard to the line located, and the papers and plans prepared by the Chief Engineer and his Assistant, the Committee desire to say, that, so far as they are able to judge, they are of the most complete and satisfactory character.

The prominent points aimed at were briefly these :—

First, to secure a supply which in the character of its works, and in the purity and abundance of its water, should be worthy of the present position of our city, and arranged with a view to its regular and rapid increase.

Second, to guard the system of expenditure so as to insure a proper and thorough construction in connection with an economical outlay, and thereby secure such a plan as should at once gratify the pride and fully meet the wants of our citizens, at the most reasonable cost.

With this intention, in all honor and with motives which challenge scrutiny, the labors of the Committee were commenced.

This duty was somewhat facilitated, and also somewhat complicated from the fact that the great importance of this question had, for a long time, attracted the attention of the public, and while on the one hand the Committee were enabled to profit from past investigation and experience, on the other, different projects having each enlisted their several adherents, it became no light task to present such a plan as should at once secure the attention and meet the approbation of all.

Of these different projects one in particular enlisted the sympathies of many of our citizens. We allude to the plan of supply from wells within, or in the vicinity of the city.

The present supply of our entire city is procured at present from these sources, and as the number of wells is very large, and the supply apparently inexhaustible, it is argued with some show of reason, that a collection of wells, or a large single well, may be so constructed, as to afford an abundant supply in our immediate vicinity, at a moderate cost. This "show of reason," however, will not bear close analysis. If the true statistics of the amount of positive inconvenience and hard labor daily suffered and expended by our citizens, who have become, by long usage, accustomed to the evil, and also of the positive impurity and unhealthiness of the water, prized *because* it is from wells, could be summed up and presented to public inspection, the aggregate results would appear almost incredible. If the noble example of the benefits of an adequate and pure supply in our sister city, were not ever present before us, ignorance on this subject might be "bliss," and without the possibility of a better state of things we might be contented with so meagre and uncertain an alternative: but the arguments ably advanced in the Report of John S. Stoddard, Esq., Document No. Nine, show, beyond question, that this method of supply cannot be thought of for municipal uses, and will not bear comparison in quantity or economy of cost, with that presented to the electors in June last.

This point being settled in the opinion of the Committee, the most prominent feature of the Plan, viz: that of the source of supply, was easily and readily determined. The provision which nature has made for our city, in the clear and beautiful ponds and streams along the southern shore of our Island, is evident to the most casual observer, and whatever pains may be taken by a few individuals to distract attention from this source, cannot be of importance to the final issue. There, and only there, if Brooklyn is to have at all, what may be dignified with the name of a supply, can it be procured. And here it is proper to say, that having in two instances rejected plans in each of which this was the prominent feature, the future action of the popular will must exercise itself simply on minor details and secondary questions.

After the adoption of this point the arrangement of the details was taken up.

In this discussion it was evident at the outset that a liberal supply was needed at present, and that in view of the approaching Consolidation with Williamsburgh and vicinity, and the rapid growth of the entire district, ample provision was necessary for the present and future. On the scale of supply in the City of New York it was ascertained that for our population there would be required at present seven millions of gallons daily, and adding to this the supply to the City, as it would rank at the time of completion of the works, the shipping, and other outlets of like character, it was decided to estimate on a present supply of not less than twenty million gallons, and to construct the works on a scale adapted to an eventual supply of forty millions of gallons daily.

With these views full and careful surveys were made, and a Final Location line staked out, from the Gate House in the Dam at Smith's Pond, on Supply Reservoir, No. 4, to the Receiving Reservoir at Baiseley's Pond, and thence to the Engine House and Distributing Reservoir. A particular description of this line with its courses and distances, tangents and curves, is given in document No. Four, and the entire work carefully plotted on the sheets of maps. The surveys were made under the direction of Gen. Burnett, and the Final Location under the personal direction of the Principal Assistant. It is based on the information acquired from the surveys of Wm. J. McAlpine, Daniel Marsh, and Thos. T. Wierman, Esquires,

Civil Engineers, of great experience, together with the observations taken at the time, and from our personal knowledge of the country, and the locating talent of the engineer in charge, we can say with perfect confidence that there is established between the extreme points the best line which can possibly be adopted. It is ready for the contractors at any time, and the test levels having been carried through in connection with it, from the Coping of the United States Dry Dock at the Navy Yard, are established on a basis of which there can be no question.

The general details of the Plan adopted are briefly these:

First, to connect a portion of Smith's Pond with the Ponds known as Pine's and L. Cornwell's, into a common Supply Reservoir, to be prepared for such use by thoroughly cleaning out all the vegetable matter down to the clean sand, under the entire water surface, and by constructing a substantial dam of earth-work and puddling of the proper height, with an ornamental dressed stone apron. This Reservoir was to be provided with a large and ornamental Gate and Keeper's House, for regulating the flow into the canal, which commenced at this point, and to be ornamented with a carriage road and fencing around the entire enclosure.

Second. To prepare as additional supply reservoirs, the three ponds west of this point known as P. Cornwell,s, Simonsons', and Nostrand's, in similar manner, connecting them by convenient lateral canals to the main canal, which was to connect Supply Reservoir No. 4 with the Receiving Reservoir at Baiseley's Pond.

Third. To make this connection by means of an open Canal, in preference to a closed Conduit, partly to avoid the injurious alternative of raising the 4th Supply Reservoir above its natural level, and thereby impeding its discharge, and partly on account of the material saving in cost, which will be very evident from an inspection of the estimates, showing a cost for 4 2-3 miles of conduit of $712,695 98, in comparison with a cost of $176,133 32, for 7 1-4 miles of open canal.

In this canal, with the cross-section adopted, the discharge, with a grade of two inches per mile, would be 35,000,000 gallons daily, being four inches less per mile than the grade required for a closed conduit.

Fourth. To enlarge the dimensions of Baiseley's Pond, by constructing its dam some distance below the present one, and to prepare it in a manner similar to the Supply Reservoirs, with the exception of the dam, which was to be of dressed stone. In this reservoir the canal terminated through a dressed stone influx chamber, and the line of conduit commenced at the gate house.

Fifth. To construct from the gate house to the pump well of the engine house, a substantial conduit of brick and stone masonry, on concrete foundations, capable of passing at a depth of five feet, with a grade of six inches per mile, forty millions of gallons daily. The flow of this conduit might be largely increased by deepening the water-way, as is done with the Croton aqueduct; but the practice of filling the conduit to the crown of the arch was deemed objectionable, and the section was made large enough to obviate this necessity. This conduit is much larger than that of the Croton, as is clearly shown on the plans submitted.

Sixth. At the Engine House, provision was made for two Cornish pumping engines, each capable of forcing ten millions of gallons daily to the Distributing Reservoir; the house itself being arranged for the reception of two additional engines when required. The details of the building and machinery are fully shown in the drawings made by Mr. McElroy, who has embodied in the latter the best pumping experience of Europe, and in the former, an edifice admirably adapted to its purpose, and highly ornamental in style.

The character of this very essential feature of the plan is believed to be beyond question.

Seventh. The site selected for the Distributing Reservoir was on the Cypress Hill, at a spot naturally adapted for the purpose, overlooking a splendid landscape, and fortunately located for distribution to the several branches of the Consolidated City, as the General Map submitted clearly shows.

This reservoir was divided into three apartments, with a joint surface of thirty acres, and a surface elevation of 172 feet above tide. At a depth of twenty feet its contents will be two hundred million gallons. Its area, with the grounds, will be forty-seven acres, and this area may be readily increased at any future time. The structures of this reservoir were to be of the most substantial and ornamental character, and the arrangement for distribution and drainage, by which both operations were controlled from a single gate house located at its centre, is not the least peculiar feature of the plan.

From the Gate House commences the system of distribution for the City, by a line of thirty-six inch main, down Fulton avenue, for the supply of Brooklyn proper.

The Committee deemed it very important to the certainty of the daily flow of the Receiving and Supply Reservoirs, that their heights should not be materially increased above their present levels. Theory and experiment both confirm them in this opinion, and by the plan now described, no additional elevations are required, except an increase of six-tenths of a foot in Baiseley's Pond; on the other hand, the surface grades, in the case of the Supply Reservoirs, are considerably lower than their present levels, and in consequence, a decided increase of flow will be realized.

The present level of the Receiving Reservoir (Baiseley's) is 8.40 feet above mean tide; the level proposed is 9 feet above tide. The present level of Supply Reservoir No. 1 (Nostrand's Pond,) is 13.60 feet above tide; No. 2 (Simonsons' Pond,) is 16.10 feet; No. 3 (P. Cornwell's Pond,) is 13.00 feet; in Supply Reservoir No. 4, the level of Pine's Pond is 12.20 feet, and of L. Cornwell's Pond, 10.50 feet, while the level proposed is 10.20 feet above mean tide.

The total area of reservoir surface embraced in this plan is three hundred fourteen and one-fourth acres, and the reservoir contents nine hundred and three millions and fifty thousand gallons. The length of conduit line is four and two-third miles, and of canal line, seven and a quarter miles; that of the line of force tubes, from the Engine House to the Distributing Reservoir, is about one mile.

On the canal line it is necessary to intersect, at occasional intervals, the streams from the ponds above named, together with several brooks, a few inches deep, and three to four feet wide. Instead of passing these by a diving culvert, or inverted syphon, as suggested in a former report, it is proposed to take them into the canal, and for this purpose, to construct on each, on the northern bank of the canal, a bulkhead, fitted with composition gates of two by three feet openings, to regulate or shut off their supply. A waste weir on the opposite bank is also built. To provide for cases where it is desirable to shut off the supply to the canal, an iron pipe of twenty-four inches diameter is laid across the canal bottom, entering the bulkhead, and fitted with a stop-cock. By opening this, and shutting the feed gates, the flow of the stream crosses the canal, and is discharged below it on the southern side. This arrangement is more particularly described under the specification for "Lateral Canals."

These are in brief the prominent features of a plan of supply, which would have been in most of these features second to none in this country, and with few equals or superiors in the world. In its purity of quality and abundance in quantity, and in the grandeur of character of the works, the Committee believe that ample consideration was paid to the present standing and future position of our City, however elevated that may be.

In determining the second essential point—viz: the method and cost of construction, the Committee very soon learned that the manner of letting contracts for public works in this country, has recently undergone a material change, so far as the relation of Corporation or Company and Contractor is concerned.

Formerly, in preparing a work for contract, it was subdivided into convenient sections and schedules of materials, and taken at higher or lower prices by various contractors, who were to execute severally the divisions entrusted to them. But every Corporation or Company has suffered numerous inconveniences from this practice, in failures of contractors to carry on those portions less profitable than others, and in the universal law of increase of final cost over the original estimates. Exceptions to this law are not numerous, and in some cases as in that of New York on the Croton aqueduct estimates, the plan approved by a vote of the people, and contracted in this way, was completed at a cost four-fold the estimate.

By the lesson of such results in practice, railroad and other companies, and contractors of high abilities and standing, have adopted the system of contracting entire works to a single party, under strict specifications and guards, and satisfactory securities, by which means the Company is ensured the complete construction of their works, without the risks and inconveniences heretofore experienced, while the contracting party carries them on to completion by his own skill and energy.

The examples of this practice are very numerous, and on works of the most important character, and it needs no elaborate argument to show that considerations of the kind mentioned, which influence the action of associations of individuals, for individual benefit, must be much more important to a corporation like that of a city, constantly subject to change and composed of individuals who represent only public interests.

With these views the Committee adopted, without hesitation, the principal of letting the entire work under a single contract, under proper and satisfactory restrictions, and recommended this course of action to the Common Council.

R

They went farther than this. After the estimates of the Chief Engineer were submitted and the probable cost of the work was known, they received and presented to the consideration of the Common Council, a proposition to construct such works agreeably to the plans, specifications, and directions, for a given sum, from one of the most energetic and responsible contracting Firms in this country, the sum being within the estimates of cost.

The Commitee have thus been enabled not only to present a plan of the most ample and satisfactory character, but also by fortunate circumstances, to demonstrate beyond any question, the reliability of the estimates for the cost of this plan, although they are less by several millions, than those of the plan presented in 1853, which was not thus guaranteed.

While the attention of the Corporate authority was directed to the Water Question, a company was organised in Williamsburg, for its supply from springs and wells. Having, from an extensive experiment, arrived at a conclusion unfavorable to this method of supply, surveys were made by the Engineer of the Company, on the northern side of the Island, to determine the practicability of introducing water from some of the lakes in that vicinity. It was found, however, that serious natural obstacles were to be encountered, which made the line objectionable, and their attention was directed to the southern side of the Island. Here they found favorable ground, and an abundance of water, and with the forethought usually characteristic of private enterprise, they immediately secured the right to those streams and lands, and in the winter of 1852-3, obtained from the Legislature, the necessary extension of their charter, to enable them to proceed with the object in view.

It appears from the papers in possession of the Committee, that ample notice was given to the authorities of this city, of their surveys and negociations. No adequate steps were however taken to secure our interests in this respect, and it is evident, that before any decisive action on the part of the City can be made, the rights of this Company must be first extinguished. Much as they regretted this state of things, the Committee did not hesitate to recommend this course, and included in their estimate, a sum which they presumed would be sufficient for this purpose.

In December 1852, a Bill was prepared for such action on the part of the Legislature (in a secret session of the Common Council,) as should authorize the City to take the necessary steps for the introduction of a supply of water. As originally prepared, the provision by which no action of the Common Council was final until approved by a vote of the people, was omitted. To meet this omission in Common Council Jan. 21, 1853, the following preamble and resolution was offered by Ald. Dayton:

Whereas, the charter of this city provides, that after the Common Council shall have determined in what manner the city shall be supplied with water, and the expense thereof, it shall be their duty to refer the matter to the people, before proceeding with any works for that purpose for their adoption or rejection;

And Whereas, by an act amendatory of the charter passed June 19th, 1851, this provision for the submission of the question to the people, was amended by authorizing the Common Council to expend a sum not exceeding three hundred thousand dollars for the purpose of purchasing land and construction of the necessary works;

And Whereas, it appears from the public prints that an act is now before the Legislature of this State, said to have been adopted by the late Common Council in secret session, proposing to create a debt of over three millions of dollars, for the purpose of prosecuting such water works, without submitting the question to the people of this city, whose interests are vitally involved in this question, and are to be effected in a lasting degree thereby.

Whereas, the whole previous action of this city has been on this subject, opposed to the creation of a large water debt, without submitting the question to the people, therefore;

Resolved—As the sense of this Common Council, that the said bill now before the Legislature, should not be enacted into law without a provision therein submitting to the people of this city, according to the original requirements of the city charter, whether said works shall be prosecuted, and the expenses thereof incurred as a public charge, and a debt created, as contemplated by said act.

Resolved—That the clerk of this board transmit forthwith copies of the foregoing preamble and resolution to the senator and members of Assembly, representing this city in the Legislature.

After a long debate the acting President, Ald. Harteau, called the question on Ald. Dayton's amendment, and on the ayes and noes being recorded, it was lost by a vote of 19 to 1. Ald. Dayton only voting in the affirmative.

In the Common Council of the City of Brooklyn, on Monday evening, Jan. 31st, an interesting discussion arose upon the water question, on submitting to the people the project for supplying the City with water, before any movement was made to enter into contracts for building water works. The discussion arose during the business order of petitions and communications, and was commenced by

Ald. Dayton, who rose and said, that as the time for reconsidering the vote which was taken on the 21st., refusing to submit the question of a supply of water for the city to the people, had gone by before he had an opportunity to present a petition to the Common Council, which was handed to him at a late hour on the evening of their last meeting, he would then present the petition, which ran as follows:

To the Honorable the Common Council of the City of Brooklyn:

The undersigned citizens and tax payers of Brooklyn, have learned that a bill is now before the Legislature, to be passed into a law, for supplying this city with water, and for that purpose authorizing the creation of a debt of over three millions of dollars.

They believe that some plan for such a supply is desirable, but they are not prepared to assent to the bill now proposed for that purpose, deeming the creation of such a debt a matter of public deliberation and determination more than has been given to it. They are desirous that the question shall be submitted to the people of this city as originally required by the City Charter for their decision, and that we have the approval of a majority of the citizens of Brooklyn, voting on the question, before any act shall be prepared.

Such a course was pursued in New York, and past experience in the history of our own city points to the necessity of caution in running into debt.

They, therefore, respectfully ask your Hon. Body to reconsider the vote by which the proposition to have such a provision inserted in the bill was rejected.

George Hall,	D. Leavitt,
C. P. Smith,	Martin Reyerson,
Henry C. Murphy,	J. Carson Brevoort,
Samuel Smith,	John G. Bergen,
Edward Copeland,	R. P. Perrin,
Joseph Sprague,	Robert Robbins,
Thos. G. Talmage,	Isaac Otis,
Francis B. Stryker,	Henry E. Pierpont,
Evan M. Johnson,	Thomas J. Gerald,
John Halsey,	N. Pearce,
Wm. S. Herriman,	D. Van Voorhis,
Wm. Ellsworth,	O. D. Burtis,
Daniel Embury,	John B. Graham,
A. G. Benson,	A. B. Crossman,
Wm. Powers,	Wm. Hunter, jr.
J. C. Delaplane,	Charles E. Bill,
S. G. Arnold,	Fisher Howe,
Joseph Dean,	Robert F. Manly,
John F. Trow,	S. Haynes,
John W. Hunter,	William Halsey,
A. Wright,	John Smith,

Edward Anthony.

After a long debate this principal was adopted unanimously.

On the 3d of June, 1853, the Legislature granted to the City a Charter under which the supply of water and the measures to be taken in connection with it were specified and authorised.

On the 7th of April, 1854, this Charter was amended by Act of the Legislature, empowering the City to do the work by contract or otherwise, and divesting the management of the work of a political aspect by increasing the number of Water Commissoners from five to six.— The Act, with its amendments, is given in Document Number Eleven.

At a special meeting of the Common Council held June 7, 1853, the order of Special Business having been taken up, Ald. Dayton, from the Special Committee appointed to purchase certain water rights, &c., reported as follows :

Purchase of rights of James Smart, deed for Pond Mill Stream, and some 44 acres of land situated on East Meadow Creek ; Deed for the Pond, Flour Mill stream, and some 5 acres of land situated on Parsonage Creek, belonging to Parmenus Smith. Deed for the pond, flour mill and stream on Hook Creek East, and belonging to Pearsall Cornwell.

The Committee have also obtained the passage of an act, entitled an act to supply the city of Brooklyn with water, a certified copy of which is herewith submitted together with the deed and abstracts.

Also, an account current of the monies received and paid out hereunto annexed, asking that the same may be received with the accompanying documents, and Committee be discharged.

CITY OF BROOKLYN.—In account with John A. Dayton, Chairman of Special Committee on purchase of water streams, &c.

Dr. To purchase East Hook Creek:
E. Cornwell.	$13,000 00
Do. Parsonage Do., P. Smith	11,500 00
Do. East Meadow, Do., J. Smart	18,360 00
Paid M. Lambertson on account	100 00
Do. Peter Nostrand on Contract	50 00
Do. J. F. Stoothoff	10 00
Do. Thomas Cornwell	25 00
Contingent expenses for the purchase of streams and obtaining passage of Water Bill at Albany	1,227 00
	$44,272 00
Balance due the City	78 00
	$44,350 00

Cr.—Warrant dated 1853		700 00
Do. From Water Account	$1,650	
" " "	4,500	
Do. Temporary Bond	1,200	18,150 00
Temporary Bond		25,000 00
Warrant		500 00
		$44,350 00

The motion for the adoption of the report was then put. Ayes 17. Carried unanimously.

PAYMENTS ON WATER ACCOUNT.

1851.
Dec. 13—Husted & Kendall,	Stage and expenses to Jamaica and Hempstead Water Committee		$47 50
16—W. J. McAlpine,	Expenditures (as per vouchers)		369 75
18—James R. Chilton,	Analysing water		60 00

1852.
Jan. 6—C. Brush, Mayor,			5 00
24—W. J. McAlpine,	Expenditures (as per vouchers)		612 02
		Carried Forward	$1,094,27

	Brought Forward	$1,094 27
Feb. 11—W. J. McAlpine,	Expenditures, (as per vouchers,)	364 59
17—John S. Stoddard,	Surveys	140 00
April 6—W. J. McAlpine,	Disbursements (as per vouchers)	202 38
20— "	" (")	726 07
May 27— "	Bill of W. A. Perkins for services	310 00
June 30—William Canfield,	Omnibus and Expenses of Common Council to Jamaica and Hempstead	71 75
July 14—W. J. McAlpine,	Payment on account of services	258 00
" "	" in full " to date	1,075 33
17— "	Disbursements (as per vouchers)	80 87
26—Artemas Whitlock,	Expenditures for guages, &c.	250 00
Aug. 4— "	Balance of expenditure for do.,	99 07
Sept. 7—Samuel F. Cogswell,	Copying water report	25 00
Oct. 19—Artemas Whitlock,	Expenditures (as per vouchers)	310 01
Dec. 7— "	" (")	146 14
" 21— "	" (")	132 27
Lambert & Lane,	Drawing paper, &c., for water works	7 81
" 24—D. M. Talmage,	Expenses going to Cornwell's Mill Pond, &c.	5 00
1853.		
Jan. 17—J. M. Van Cott,		250 00
" —Artemas Whitlock,	Services and Expenditures	144 21
Feb. 23—Isaac Van Anden,	Printing Water Reports, &c.	402 75
Mar. 15—J. M, Van Cott,	Contingent Disbursements	500 00
April 30—Howard C. Cady,	Services on the Water Business	250 00
May 3—John A. Dayton,	Contingent Disbursements	700 00
" 10— "	Purchase of Lands for Reservoir	1,650 00
" 26— "	Contingent Disbursements	500 00
June 2—J. M. Van Cott,	Services on the Water Account	750 00
" 18—N. F. Waring,	" " in part	87 55
" 23— "	" " balance in full	162 45
July 15—E. A. Lambert,	Payment of Sundry Expenses water election	200 00
" 16—E. Estabrook, Comptroller,	" " "	975 00
" 22—I. Van Anden,	Printing Bill	116 00
" 29—A. H. Osborne,	Services and Expenses relative to water law	50 00
C. H. Thompson,	Balance to Inspectors, &c., Water Election	25 00
Aug. 3.—E. B. Spooner,	Printing Bill	18 75
" 6—William Foulkes,	Advertising Water Works and Election	38 30
J. W. Heighway,	" Plans and Election	37 00
Lewis Cornell,	Room Hire, Second District, Fourth Ward, Water Election	15 00
" 31—Brooklyn Bank,	Payment of temporary Water Bonds and interest	27,116 66
Sept. 7— "	" " "	12,236 71
" 9—Commiss. of Sinking Fund,	" " "	4,590 25
	Carried Forward	$56,114 29

		Brought Forward	$56,115 29
" 30—Albert Powell,	Fitting up polls at Armory for Water Election		10 00
James H. Howe,	Room hire, 1st District, 1st Ward, "		15 00
Oct. 7—W. H. Noe,	Fixtures for Water Election		19 38
Joseph Hegeman,	Room hire, 1st District, 4th Ward		15 00
Coit & Brothers,	" " 3d "		20 00
John Muchmore,	" " 10th "		15 00
Burtis & Smith,	" " 11th "		15 00
James Wiber,	" 62 Atlantic street		15 00
Greeley & McElrath,	Advertising Water Loan		12 80
5—Edward Rowe,	Room hire, Water Election, 2d District, Seventh Ward		20 00
7—Wm. Seaman,	Fitting up polls for election, 1st District, Seventh Ward		9 35
15—C. B. Holder,	Room hire for election, 9th Ward		10 00
25—I. Van Anden,	Printing, &c.		165 21
28—W. C. Bryant,	Advertising Water Loan		3 75
Nov. 2—William Foulkes,	" "		4 60
26—O. D. Burtis,	Room hire for Water Election, First District, First Ward		15 00
Dec. 2—John G. Lambertson,	Searches and Costs in the matter of water property		735 00
Dec. 30—M. Evans & S. Graham	Expenses to from and at Albany,		125 00
1854.			
Feb. 22—Henry Foster, Collector,	Taxes on Water Property		200 81
April 14—Hallock, Butler & Hall,	Advertising Water Loan,		6 12
May 15—John A. Dayton, Chairman,	Sundry Expenses,		905 82
16—Joseph Soper,	School Tax on Water Property in Hempstead,		33 81
28—J. W. Heighway,	Printing Report of J. S. Stoddard, on well system		25 00
June 13—Inspectors & Clerks,	Services at Water Election, June 1st.		1,200 00
Thomas Byrnes,	Room Hire " 3rd dist. 5th ward,		10 00
July 8—F. A. Morrell,	" " 1st " 11th "		10 00
Albert Powell,	" " 1st " 3rd "		10 00
P. V. C. Langdon,	" " 1st " 1st "		10 00
Coit & Bro's,	" " 2nd " 3rd "		10 00
A. O. Millard,	" " 3rd " 11th "		10 00
John Weber,	" " 2nd " 5th "		10 00
J. Cornell,	" " 2nd " 4th "		10 00
A. Blake,	" " 2nd " 1st "		10 00
S. H. Cahoone,	" " 1st " 10th "		10 00
Henry T. Taber,	" " 1st " 5th "		10 00
James Wiber,	" " 1st " 6th "		10 00
" 11—Patrick Balfe,	" " 2nd " 7th "		10 00
Stone & Weeks,	" " 2nd " 2ud "		10 00
" 17—Richard Butt,	" " 9th "		10 00
" 20—Ward B. Burnett,	Services and surveys in relation to Water,		2,397 65
		Carried Forward	$62,258 49

		Brought Forward	62,258 49
" 29—I. Van Anden,	Printing Reports,	. . .	263 82
Aug. 1—J. W. Heighway,	Printing Water Report,	. . .	63 50
Wm. H. Noe,	Fitting up Rooms for Water Election,	.	5 09
Litchfield & Co.,	Candles for Water Election,	. .	14 40
P. P. Foote,	Room Hire 3rd dist. 4th ward,	. .	10 00
			$62,615 30

I hereby certify the above to be a correct transcript from the books of this office, and of the whole of expenditure upon said account.

E. EASTABROOK,
Comptroller.

COMPTROLLER'S OFFICE,
Dec. 20, 1854

RECEIPTS TO WATER ACCOUNT.

1851.
Dec. 2d, Transfer from Contingent Fund, ... 3,000 00
1852.
June 30.   do   "   do   . . , . . . 1,283 07
July 31.   do   "   do 1,000 00
Dec. 31.   do   "   do 250 00
1853.
January 31. do.   "   do 250 00
Feb. 28.   do.   "   do 4,750 00
June 23.   Re-transfer of monies borrowed by temporary bond . . 1,650 00
Aug 22.   Premium and Interest on Bonds sold 3,021 24
Sept. 7.   Interest received on Bond sold 295 00
Dec. 12.   John A. Dayton, Chairman Special Committee
    Bal. Cash unexpended, returned with vouchers . . 78 00
1854.
July 1.   Pearsall Cornwell, Rent of Water Property, . . . 250 00
    Proceeds of Bonds Sold; credited to Bond Account . . 55,000 00

$70,827 31

I certify the above to be a correct transcript from the accounts in the office and of the whole of the receipts to said account.

E. EASTABROOK,
Comptroller's Office, Dec. 21, 1854.   Comptroller.

The Committee cannot close this Report without some allusion to the course of the Canvass preceding the Water Election of June 1st, by which the plan described in the foregoing pages was rejected by a majority of the electors voting.

Some allusion has already been made to the difficulty of concentrating on any special plan, the approbation of those whose sympathies are enlisted on plans which have a different basis. The persons included under this head, voted against the plan proposed, and will vote against any plan proposed which does not embody their peculiar theories.

Another class of our citizens are opposed to any water plan, on the ground of increased expense and taxation, and so long as they overlook the counterbalancing benefits, in the income of the works, reduced insurance, greater individual and public convenience, security health and prosperity, they will continue to oppose any plan, however short-sighted may be their policy.

The motives of the classes named are, however, more or less justifiable, and if the opposition had been confined to them, the Committee and the City would have less cause to regret the result; but the most casual observer of the interests which brought about this defeat, must have noticed how much more powerful was the combination of scheming politicians, private jealousies, and personal interests, against this project, so securely guarded for the public welfare.

It was said that the streams mentioned were "green and stagnant" in the summer, and could not be depended on for a supply;—that the Common Council wished to sell the City to Welles & Co., and the Long Island Water Works Co., without prospect of a return;—that no surveys had been made, no plans drawn, no reliable estimates submitted; and that the Water Committee had originated a gigantic swindle under the bribery of interested parties. Such charges as these were made not only in the streets and by-ways, but echoed in their Common Council Chamber, by those who would not inform themselves as to the truth of the assertions. So strongly were these assertions pressed and reiterated, that the originators and those who heard them finally came to believe them, and there is no doubt that many a vote was given adverse to the Water Plan, under the conscientious impression that the voter was rebuking a formidable imposition, and vindicating the sacred principles of public honor. Under similar and erroneous impressions, some of our most prominent and worthy citizens permitted their names to be publicly used in this quixotical crusade.

The daily newspapers teemed with statements and counter statements, plans and counter plans, personal attack and defence, which now, in the moment of cool and calm reflection, must be to many a source of unavailing regret. What has been said and done may be forgiven, and may in time be forgotten, but it cannot be obliterated. There seems to be a general impression that a public servant is not under the same control of conscience, and not as sensitive to personal honor and the good opinion of his neighbors, as the same individual in private life; that temptations are more powerful, and resistance less easy; and under this impression, the great principle of our statutes, that an accused person must be held as innocent until proved guilty, is summarily reversed, public officers being too often suspected without accusation and condemned without trial. This is particularly the case where such officers have the control of affairs connected with public expenditures, and a voice in the disposal of contracts; for where the proposal of one person is accepted, there are many rejected. To gratify one, the many must be offended, or will be, whatever the circumstances may be, and will not hesitate to make reasonable or unreasonable accusations. Those, however, who are familiar with public life and its peculiar rewards of this kind, sooner or later find that justice may be delayed, but cannot be fully arrested, and that time, which brings much of the truth to light, eventually will establish the uprightness of honorable intentions, and conscientious acts. The appeal from Philip drunk to Philip sober, is often necessary in these days of hasty judgement.

In the statements freely and openly made to influence the public mind adversely to public interests, invective language was not spared. Handbills, circulars, and newspaper columns, called on the electors to vote down the "Infamous Water Plot of the Common Council." These the Committee do not care to notice further; but there was one circular among others of its class, which is here given as a specimen of the more dignified course of opposition, and which bears the sanction of some honorable names. It is quoted with brief remarks, suggested by the communication itself.

"WATER PLAN ELECTION-

" *To the Electors of the City of Brooklyn:*

"You are called upon to deposit your vote, on Thursday, the first day of June next, in favor of or against the Water Plan submitted to you by the Common Council.

"The undersigned, *after full inquiry and examination* in relation to the said plan—the manner in which it has been brought before you, and the probable motives of the persons who seem most active in their efforts to secure a majority vote in favor of it—being decidedly opposed to its adoption, deem it proper to submit to you some of the reasons for their opposition, and ask your co-operation in defeating the same.

"1. *Taxation* upon property and *Rents paid by Tenants*, always have and must continue to *increase* in proportion to the public debt of the city. If a $4,500,000 debt be incurred, it will make the taxes about one half more than they are now: if an $8,000,000 debt be incurred, it will nearly or quite double present taxation, and as a necessary consequence, proportionally increase rents. And we are satisfied that before the proposed work shall be completed, its cost will be nearer $8,000,000 than $4,500,000; and should the plan fail to give us the water promised, in quality and quantity, its effects would be most disastrous to our city."

"Full inquiry and examination" would have shown the authors of this circular in the first place, that the expenditure of $4,500,000 is positively limited to that sum by the charter, and that the estimate of the Committee, and the principle adopted of doing the work under a single contract, endorsed by a *bona fide* proposal of reliable men, places the amount of necessary expenditures beyond a cavil. It would also have shown that this work was to be paid for by the city, by the proceeds of bonds running from 15 to 40 years, and that instead of an increased tax, the income of the Water Works would immediately after completion be not less than 6 per cent., with a probable increase to 10 per cent. At such an expenditure the city could not make a better investment. It will also be observed in the proposition of H. S. Welles & Co., that a daily supply of twenty million gallons is a part of the contract which they proposed to make, and this guarantee places this point beyond argument, so far as expenditures are concerned, or any failure of plans.

" 2. We are satisfied that the mill-pond water, for drinking and culinary purposes, is far inferior to the present well waters of this city. It is not used for such purposes by persons residing along the margins of the ponds."

The Report of General Burnett anticipates and fully rebuts this assertion, by giving the analysis of both the "mill-pond water" and the most public city wells. The chemist who made the analysis did not know whence the samples came, and his report shows a comparative purity in favor of the former, in one case 38 times, and in the most favorable case 5 1-2 times that of the latter.

" 3. Doubts have been expressed by many of our most intelligent citizens whether a sufficient supply can be had from said ponds, especially in the dry summer months.

" 4. There is strong evidence, giving reasonable certainty that an abundant supply of the *purest spring water* can be had from the well springs of the Island, at various places near the city, *in our own county*. Such was the opinion of the late lamented Major Douglass, deceased—an experienced practical engineer—as reported to the Common Council, after *careful examinations* made by him, at their request; and such is the opinion *expressed in the late report* of Mr. Burnett, the engineer employed by the Water Committee, as lately published in pamphlet, with the report of said Committee. Mr. Burnett says the water from the Main Spring of the Island, beyond the limits of a compact population, " *is remarkably pure in quality and abundant in quantity.*"

" 5. The probable expense of procuring this pure water would not exceed one-quarter, or at most, two-thirds of the sum proposed to be expended in an effort to obtain the pond water.

" 6. If the proposed plan be adopted, the whole cost of the experiment must be charged to the present city of Brooklyn; and should it fail to give the water, Williamsburgh and Bushwick would be relieved from paying any part of it, and would be built up and improved while Brooklyn improvement would be greatly diminished, if not entirely cease for many years."

If it is true that doubts of a sufficient supply were expressed, it is very certain that the evidence of interested and disinterested parties, accumulated during the very severe drought of last summer, throws some doubt over the intelligence of the doubters. If the drought alluded to, which was without precedent for a long term of years, did no other good, it settled this point beyond any further intelligent doubts and " full inquiries."

Paragraph No. 4 revives the Well supply, which probably needs no further arguments than those contained in the preceding pages. No surveys were made by Major Douglass, and the assertion that General Burnett confirms the opinion of an abundant supply " in this county," is not true in point of fact. By his Report, it is necessary to collect the discharges of the main spring along the coast, at a low level, for a continuous distance of twelve miles, to procure twenty million gallons daily supply.

Paragraph No. 5 does not show very accurate " examination " of the item of cost, leaving as it does a wide range between one-fourth and two-thirds of four and a half millions of dollars.

It would be difficult to find responsible contractors willing to contract on such an estimate, and guarantee the supply. This estimate is thus made, however, and introduces the following comment on that of the Committee.

7. "The action and proceedings of some portion of the Common Council, and especially of at least one member of the Water Committee—their apparent coalition with persons interested in the Williamsburgh Water Company, in favoring a purchase from said Company of their grounds, &c., for the sum of $150,000, and of contracting the entire work to Welles & Co., at their own bid for it, and other circumstances, have been such as not to command the confidence or respect of the public; but, on the contrary, to create just apprehensions that the $4,500,000 estimate may not have been made upon the most reliable information or solid basis. It is notorious that persons interested in the Williamsburgh Water Company, who used strong efforts to prevent the adoption of the plan submitted at a late election, are now most active in trying to secure the adoption of the present plan. Then they hoped to drive the city into a subscription to the stock of their Company; and now, after they have failed to secure sufficient public confidence in their proposed work to enable them to sell their stock, they seek to compel the city to purchase of them, at the enormous price of $150,000, their grounds and reservoir lands, which to them are, for the purpose intended, valueless.

"Finally, we ask your careful attention to this matter before you deposite your votes, and not to fail to vote against this plan under the supposition that there are comparatively few who will vote for it.—Some of the persons favoring this plan have a deep pecuniary interest to have it adopted, and have been extensively and actively, and rather secretly than publicly, engaged to accomplish their object, long before the Common Council determined to submit this plan to you, and we have reason to believe, that neither time, labor, nor expense will be spared by them in their efforts at the coming election.

Hon. JOHN DIKEMAN,
" CONKLIN BRUSH.
" FRANCIS B. STRYKER,
" EDWARD COPELAND,
" JOSEPH SPRAGUE,
" SAMUEL SMITH,
EVAN M. JOHNSON,
WILLIAM H. CARY,
JOHN J. STUDWELL,
JOHN BLUNT,
JOHN E. CAMMEYER,
FRANCIS SPIES,
BERNARD JOHNSON,
L. C. McPHAIL, M.D.
PETER G. TAYLOR,
THOMAS W. BIRTSELL,
SAMUEL SWALM, M.D.

Dated May 26, 1854.

With regard to the personal charges pointedly made in the above paragraph, we have to remark that if the "full inquiry and examination" has been made as asserted, the persons issuing this circular must have in their possession full and complete proof of what they so publicly state, and they owe it to themselves as self-constituted censors, and to the community they are anxious to protect, to make the proof as public as the charges. Nothing less than this can meet the demands of ordinary justice, or protect them from the charge of wilful misrepresentation.

This circular was very widely circulated, and did much to influence the public mind. Of the names attached to it there were some, who have, by a long life of usefulness, won the respect of our citizens. The Committee cannot believe that this subject was fully understood by them at the time of its issue, which was at the warmest period of the canvass, or that they would permit their names to be used in this way, except under an erroneous impression of the truth. Those who have passed through the trying scenes of a long and active life with untarnished reputation, must have learned to value the precepts of the golden rule, and must have observed how difficult it is to remove the breath of suspicion or the memory of a slander, however unfounded either may be. Those who heedlessly or wantonly trifle with the reputation of a fellow-citizen, offend not only themselves, but the community in which they live.

The Committee being about to surrender the charge which has been for the past year entrusted to them, respectfully submit the documents accompanying this Report, as the result of their labors and the best evidence of their interest in so important an undertaking. They feel assured that no further testimony is required to place their efforts in a proper light. They have made the only decision which prudence, sound judgment, and a true desire for the welfare of the city dictated, and recommended a course which would have secured an inestimable benefit, under some circumstances which they would gladly have changed, if possible, but which did not warrant their rejection of the general plan. However they may have been misrepresented and misunderstood, they have the testimony of a good conscience and the certainty of eventual justice.

These things were not done in secret. The Report of March 13th, 1854, was freely distributed, and contained an ample statement of the principle adopted. The plans and surveys were publicly exhibited and explained. At a meeting of the Common Council, several weeks previous to the Election, the principle of contracting proposed by the Committee was adopted, and the work directed to be thrown open for competion, but on the day of Election the majority were unfavorable to the plan, and it now becomes our duty to deposit in the archives of the city, the information accumulated on this subject.

In doing this we cannot but express the hope that the succeeding Committee may find a more cordial co-operation on the part of our citizens, and that the necessities of our city may be soon relieved by the introduction of an adequate and pure supply of water,—at no greater cost than that included in the preceeding statements.

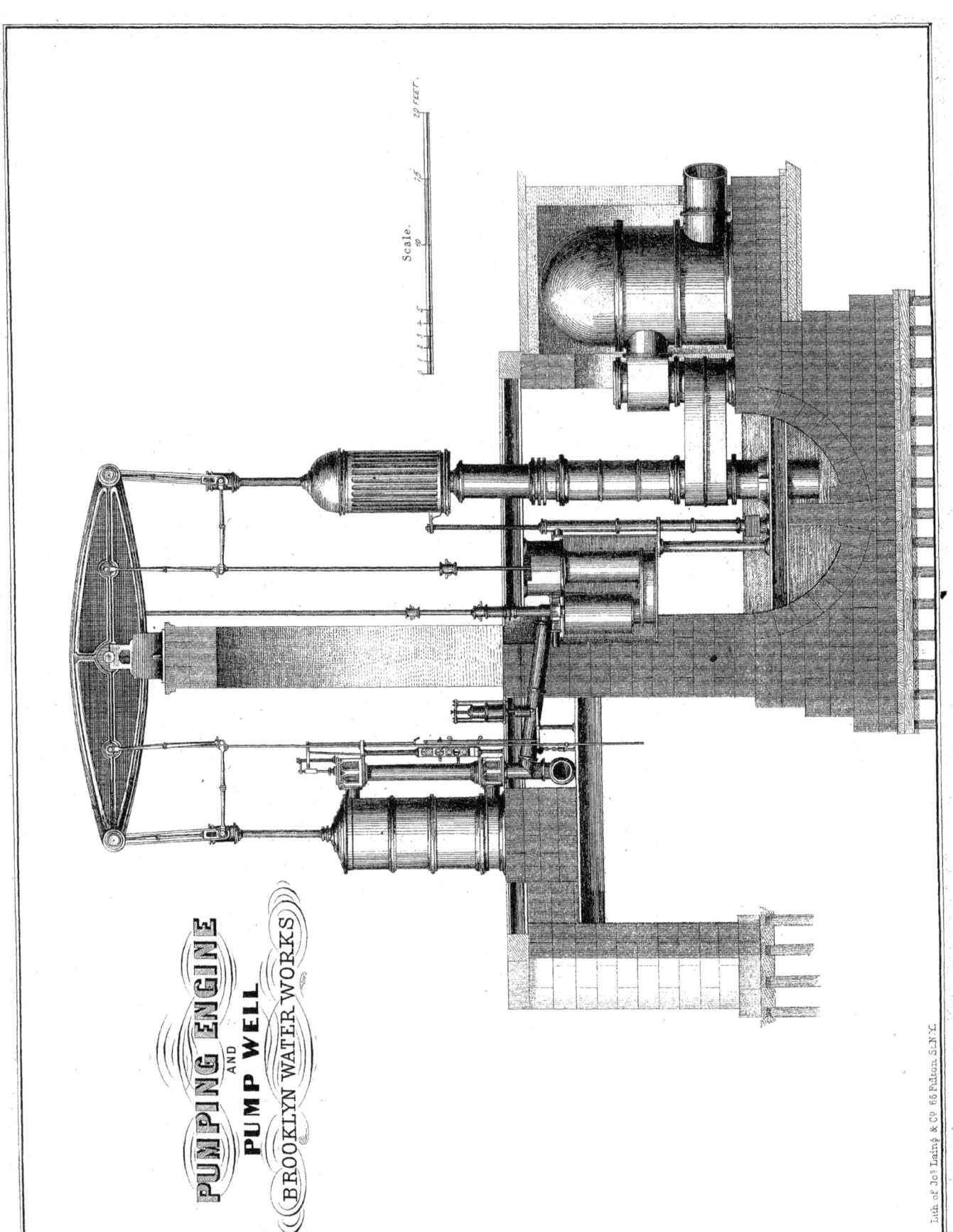

Maps and Plans

FOR THE

BROOKLYN WATER WORKS

SUBMITTED

MAY 1854.

Gen.! Ward B. Burnett,
Chief Engineer.

Samuel McElroy,
Prin. Ass.^t Engineer.

WATER COMMITTEE:

John A. Dayton, Chairman.
B. C. Brainard, D. P. Barnard,
E. G. Quevedo, Saml Booth.

MAPS:

General Map.
Distributing Map.
Conduit Line ———— Sheet N° 1.
————do———— do 2.
Canal do. ———— 3.
————do. ———— 4.
————do. ———— 5.
Distributing Reservoir
Receiving do
Storing " " N° 1.
————do————————", 2.
————", ", 3.
————", ", 4.

PLANS:

Keepers House, Distributing Reservoir, Elevation.
Gate House ———— do ———— do ———— & Plan.
" " Plan of Well.
Carriage Entrances, Elevation.
Engine House
" " Plan and Section.
Pumping Engine, Elevation.
Dam and Apron.
Road Bridge.
Farm "
Creek Culverts.
Box do
Waste Weir, Conduit.
do Canal.
Sections, Conduit and Canal.
Gate and Keepers House.

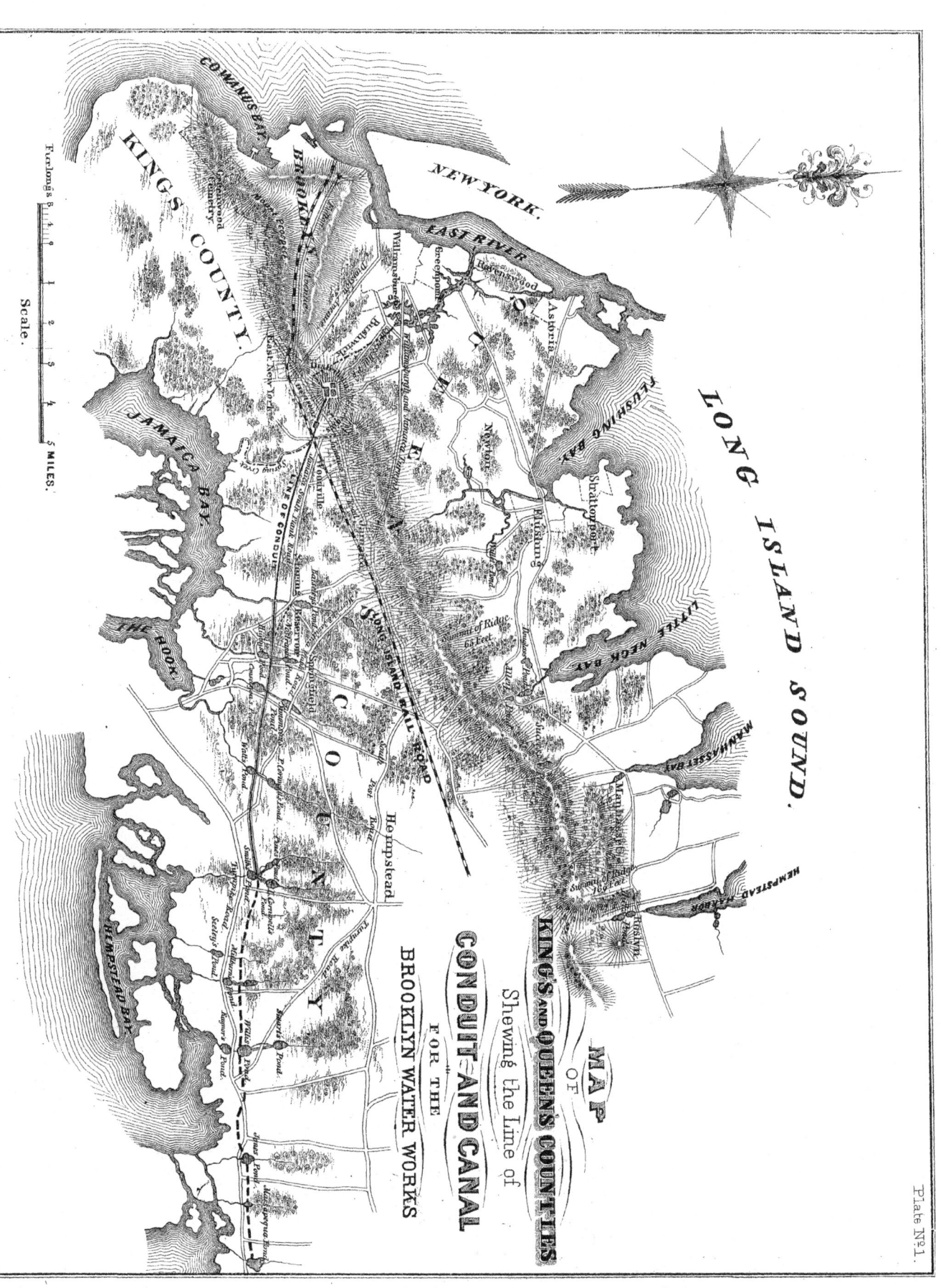

MAP OF CONDUIT AND CANAL LINE
BROOKLYN WATER WORKS
1854
SHEET N° 1.

Total length of Force Pipe ——— 1 Mile 180 Feet.
  „   „   „ Conduit ———— 4 „ 319.5 Feet.
  „   „   „ Open Canal 7 „ 1314 „
Grade of Conduit. From Baiseleys to Spring Creek. 6 in. Per Mile.
Grade of Open Canal. From Baiseley's to Smith's Road. 2 in. Per Mile.
  „   „   „   „   Spring Creek to Engine House. Level.
NOTE: The Figures on vertical lines of Profile denote cut & bone grade.

PROFILE:

Horizontal Scale:
Vertical Scale:

Plate N° 2.

MAP OF CONDUIT AND CANAL LINE
BROOKLYN WATER WORKS
1854
SHEET No. 2

Plate No. 3.

MAP OF
CONDUIT AND CANAL LINE
BROOKLYN WATER WORKS
1854
SHEET N° 3

Plate N° 4.

Lith. of Jos. Laing & Co. 66 Fulton St. N.Y.

MAP OF
CONDUIT AND CANAL LINE
BROOKLYN WATER WORKS
1854
SHEET Nº 4

Plate Nº 5.

Lith. of Jos. Laing & Co. Fulton St. N.Y.

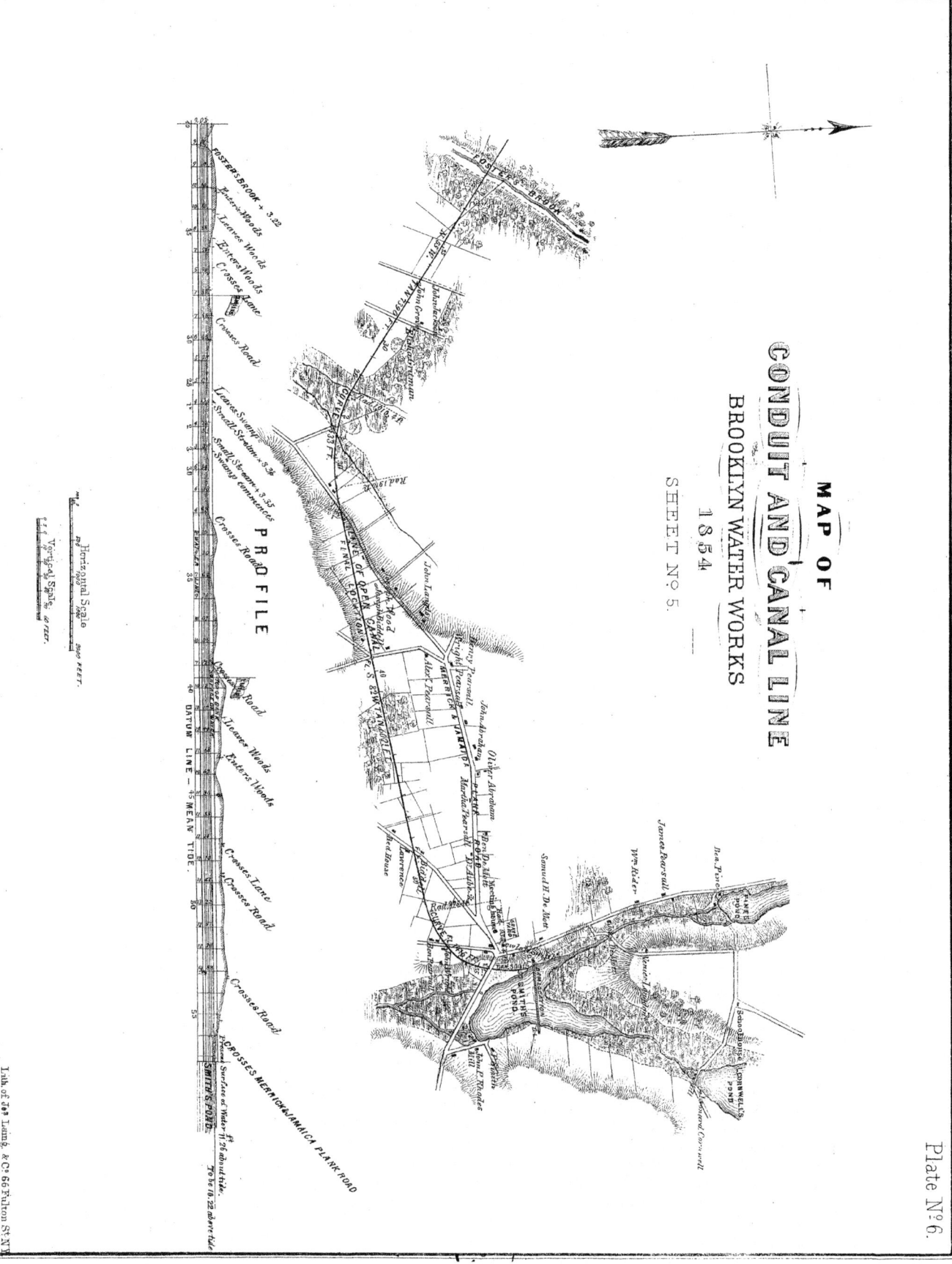

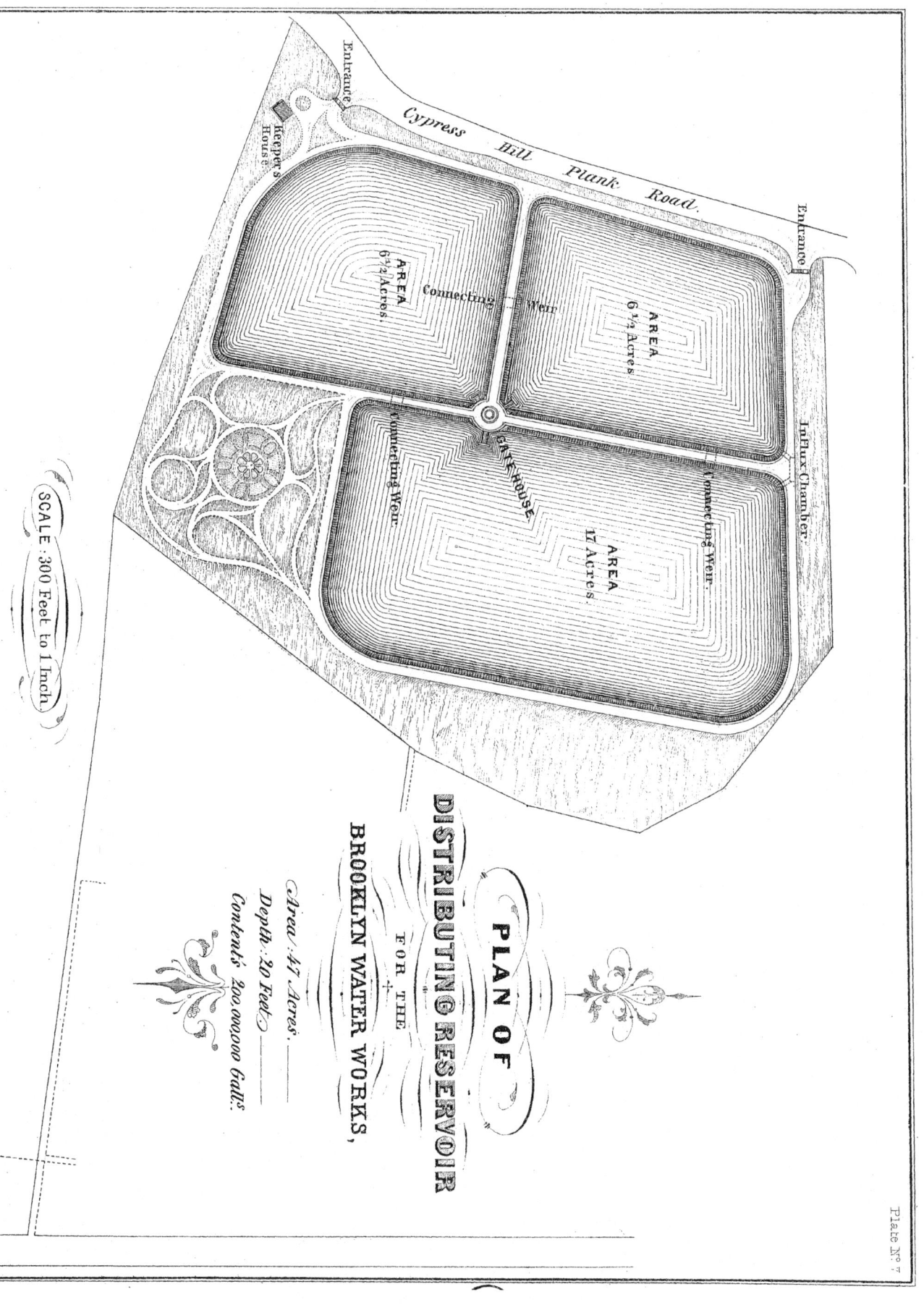

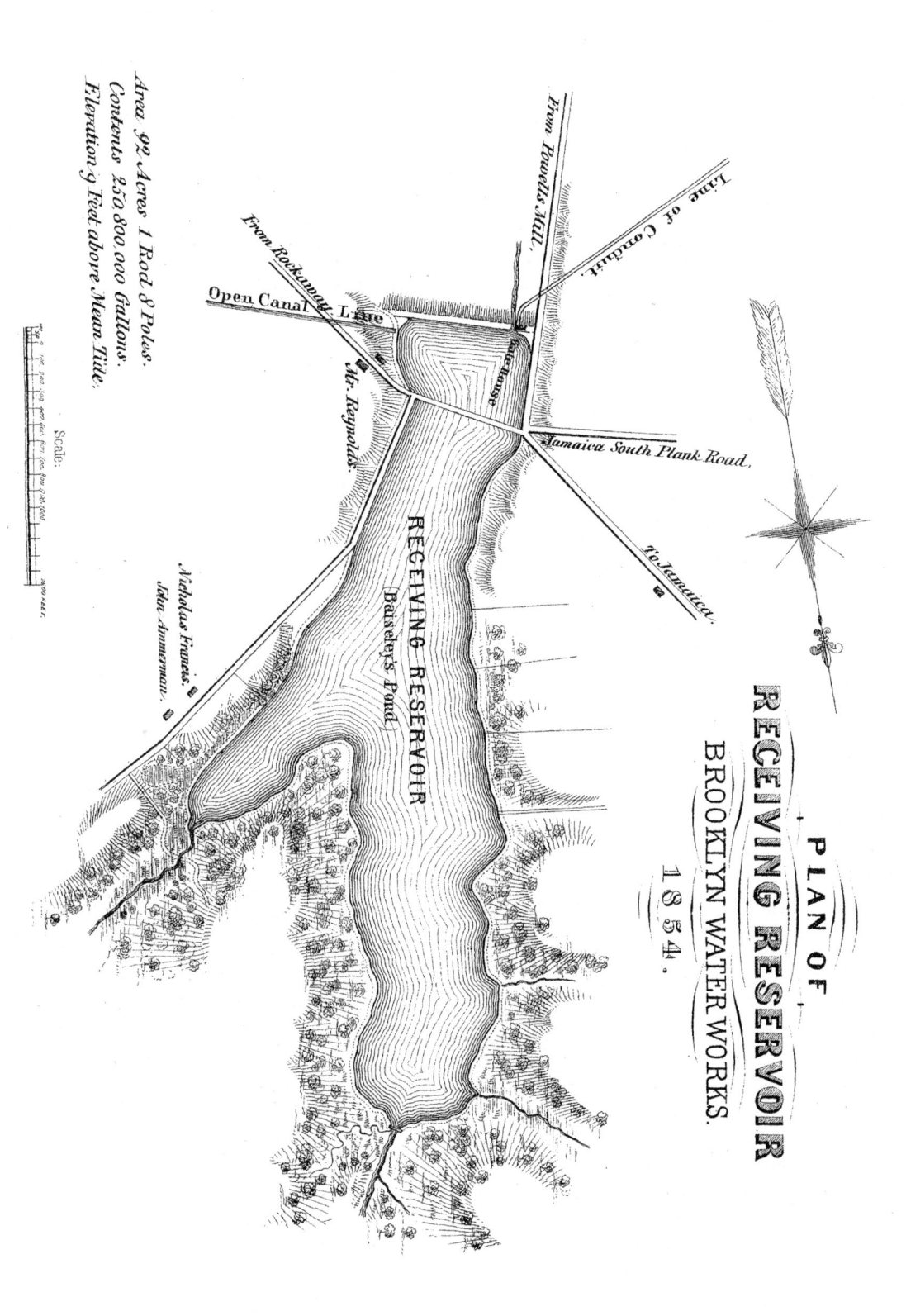

SUPPLY RESERVOIR Nº 1.
PETER NOSTRAND'S POND
BROOKLYN WATER WORKS
1854.

Area 10¼ Acres.
Contents: 24,250,000 Galls.

Doetling House.
Mill
Merrick & Jamaica Plank Road.
Springfield Hall.

Scale of Chains.

Lith. of Jos. Laing & Cº 66 Fulton St. N.Y.

Plate Nº 9.

SUPPLY RESERVOIR Nº 2.
DANIEL SIMONSON'S POND
BROOKLYN WATER WORKS
1854.

Area 12 Acres.
Contents: 24,500,000 Galls.

Plate Nº 10.

Scale of Chains

Labels on map: Dwelling House, Mill, Waste Way, Lateral Canal, Gate House, MERRICK & JAMAICA PLANK ROAD.

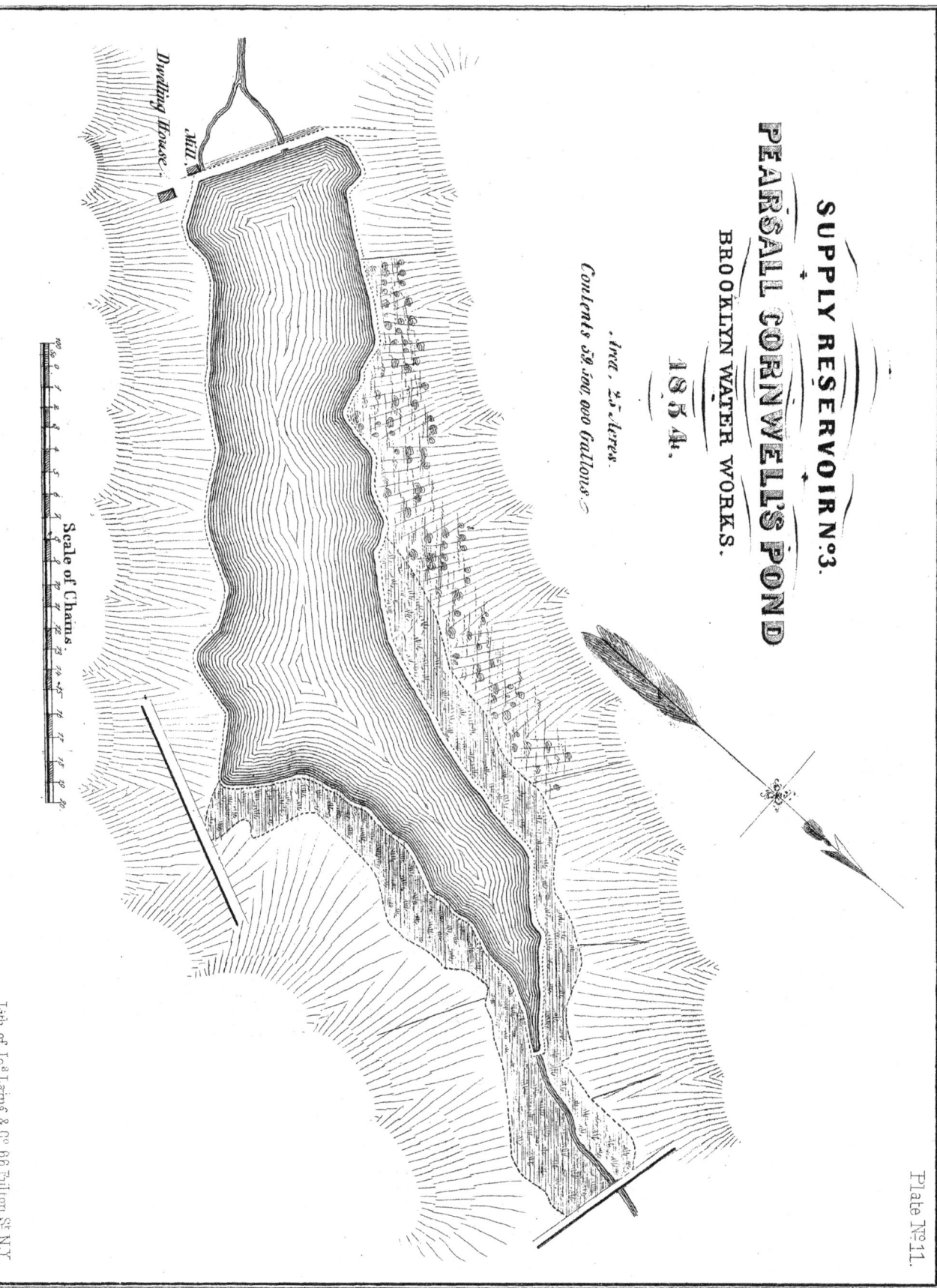

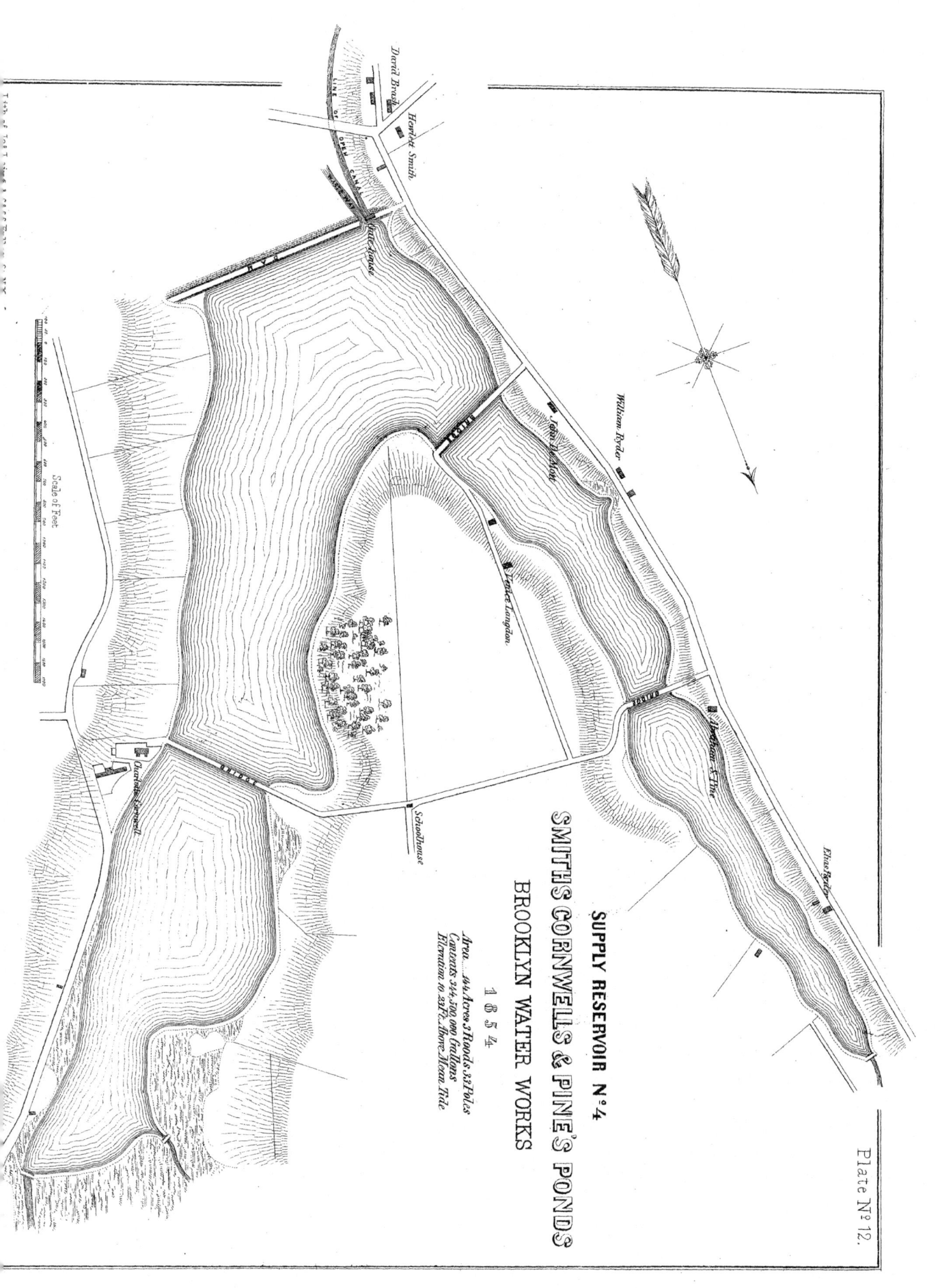

KEEPERS HOUSE
AT THE
DISTRIBUTING RESERVOIR
FOR THE
BROOKLYN WATER WORKS.

Lith. of Jos Laing & Co 86 Fulton St N.Y.

Scale:

Plate No 13

Plate No. 14.

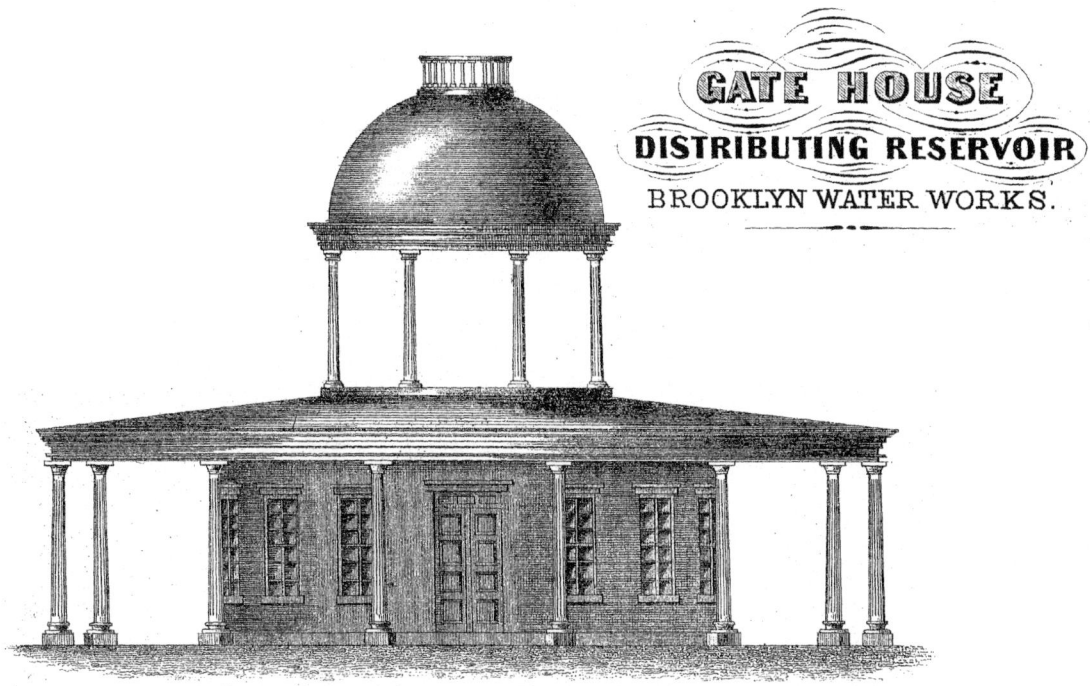

GATE HOUSE
DISTRIBUTING RESERVOIR
BROOKLYN WATER WORKS.

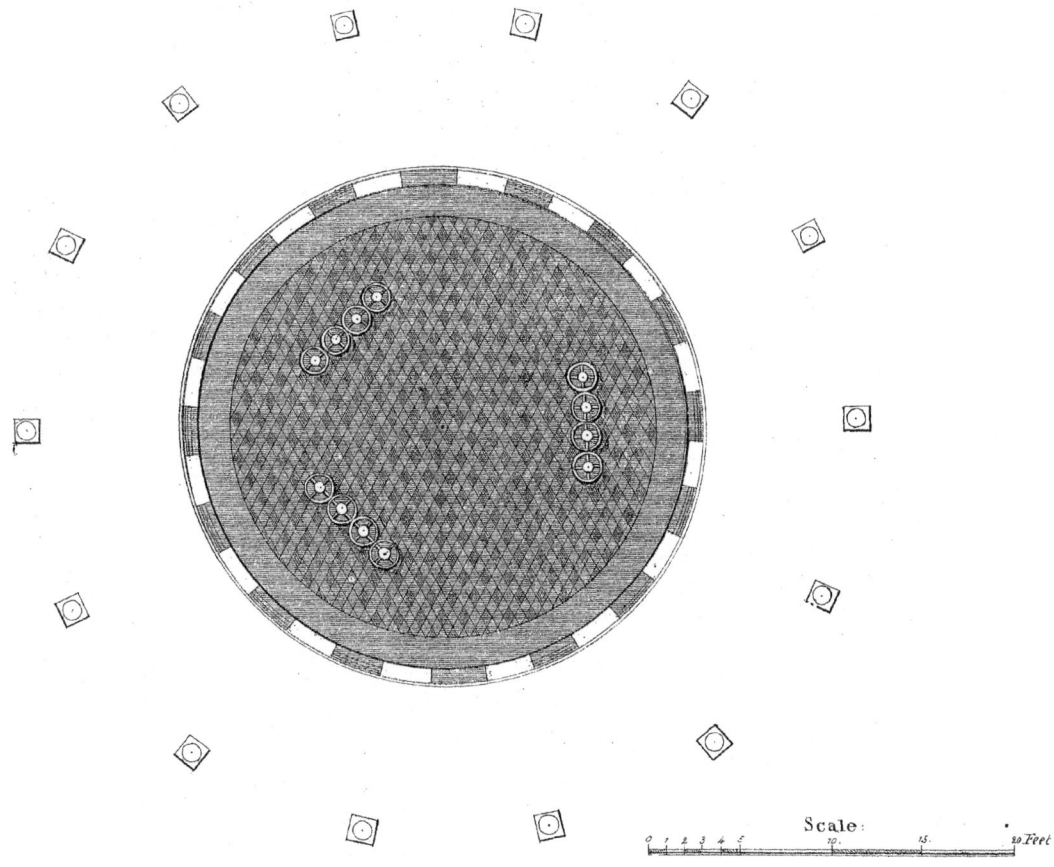

Scale
0 1 2 3 4 5   10   15   20 Feet

Lith. of Jos. Laing & Co. 66 Fulton St. N.Y.

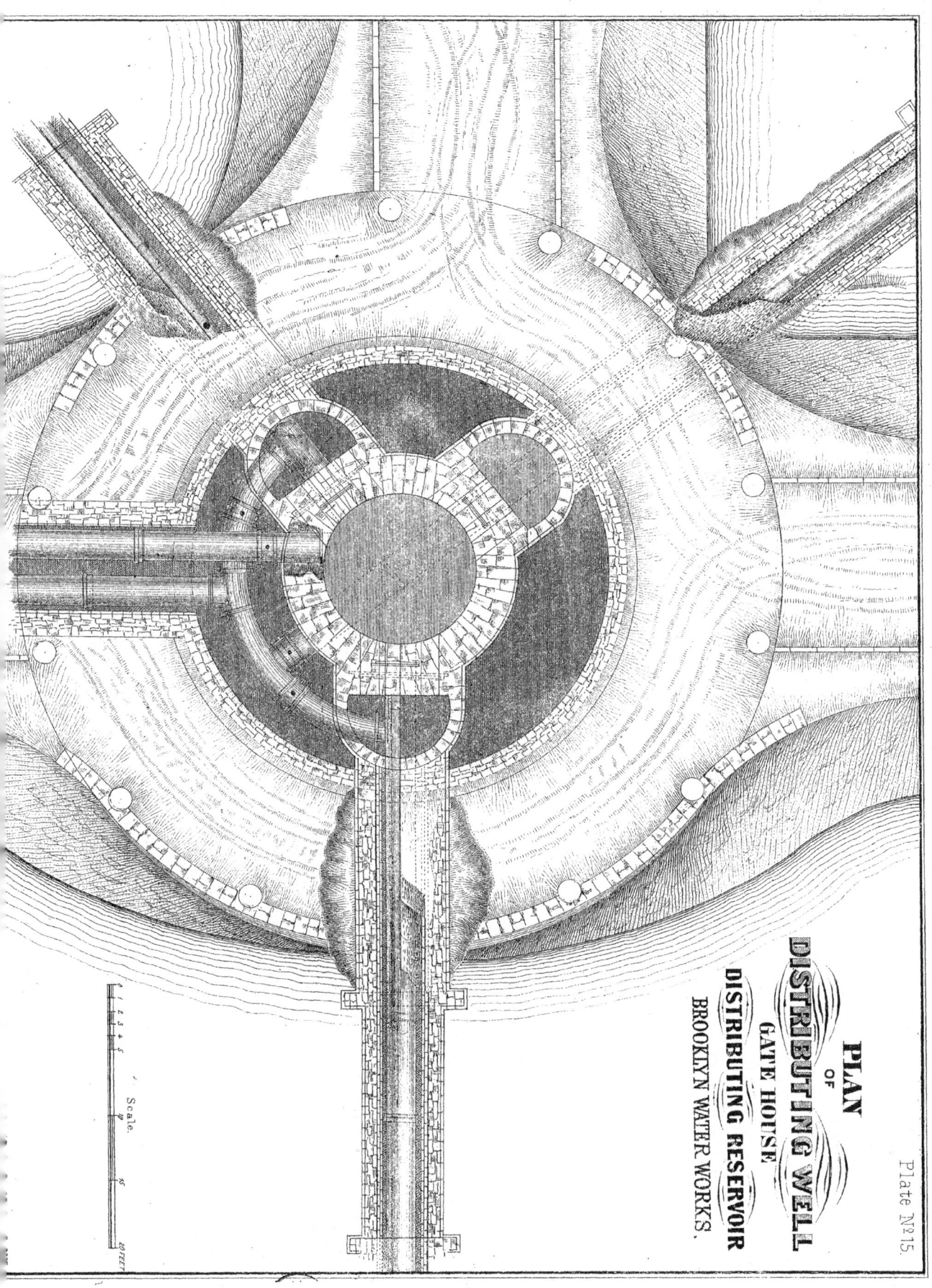

PLAN OF DISTRIBUTING WELL GATE HOUSE
DISTRIBUTING RESERVOIR
BROOKLYN WATER WORKS.

Plate No. 15.

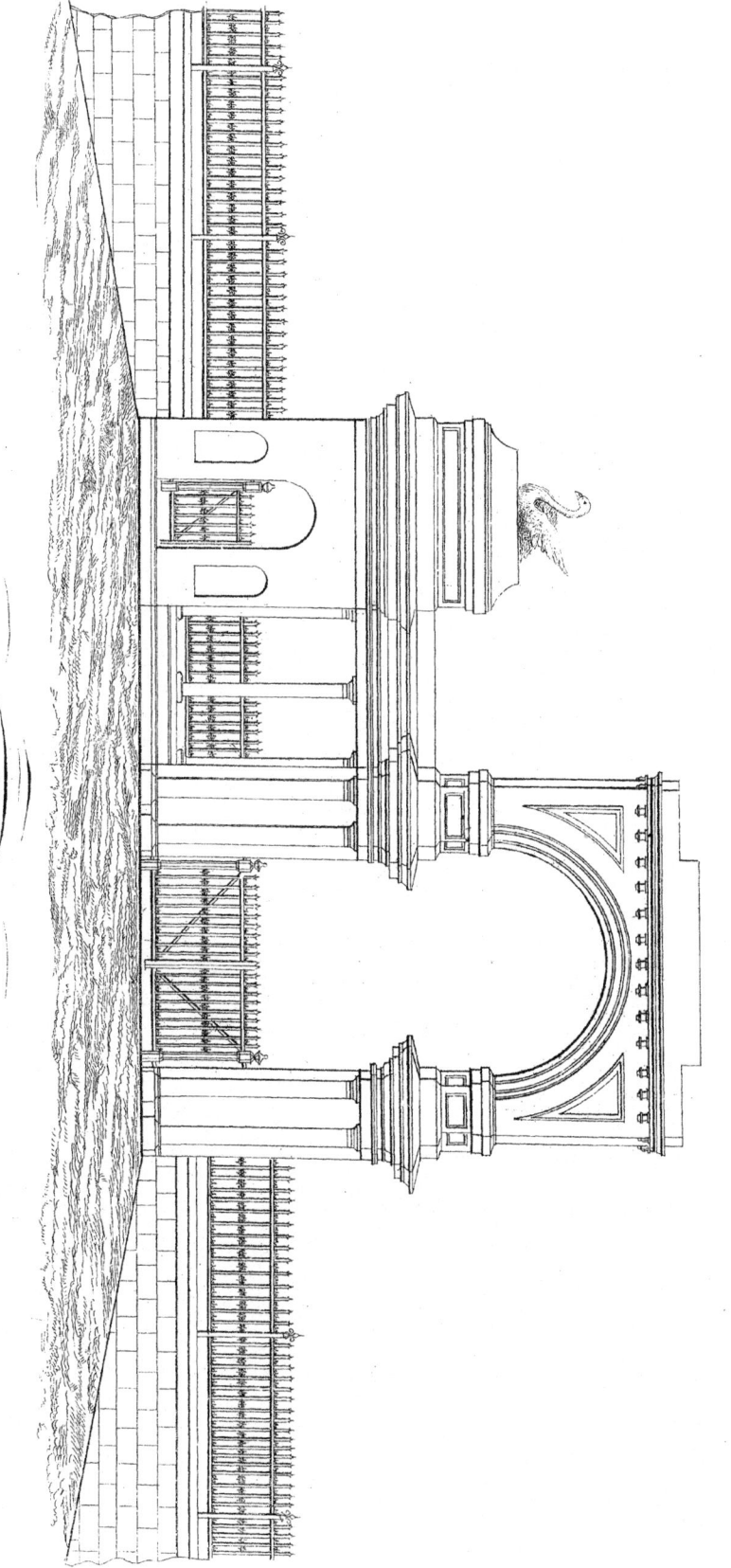

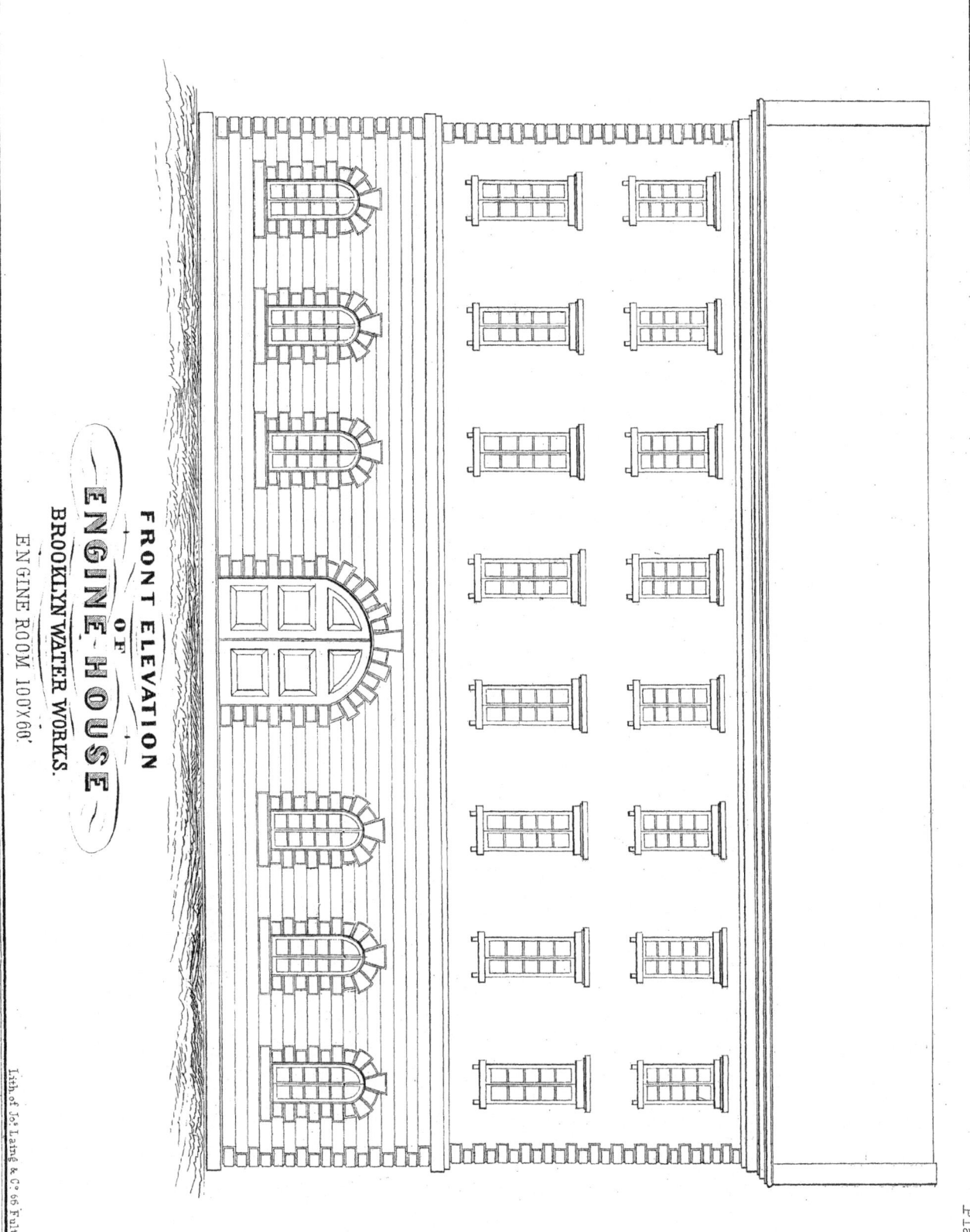

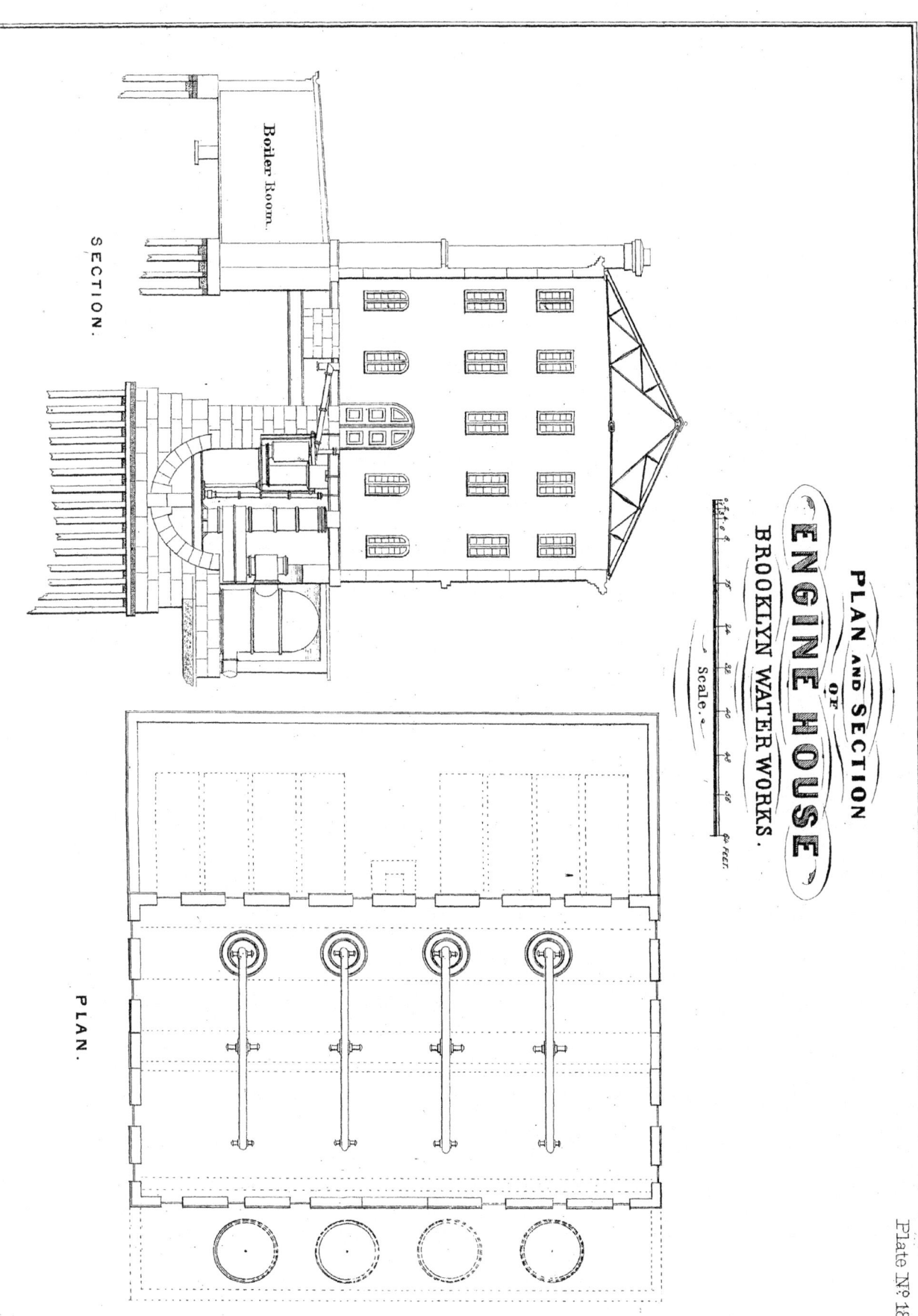

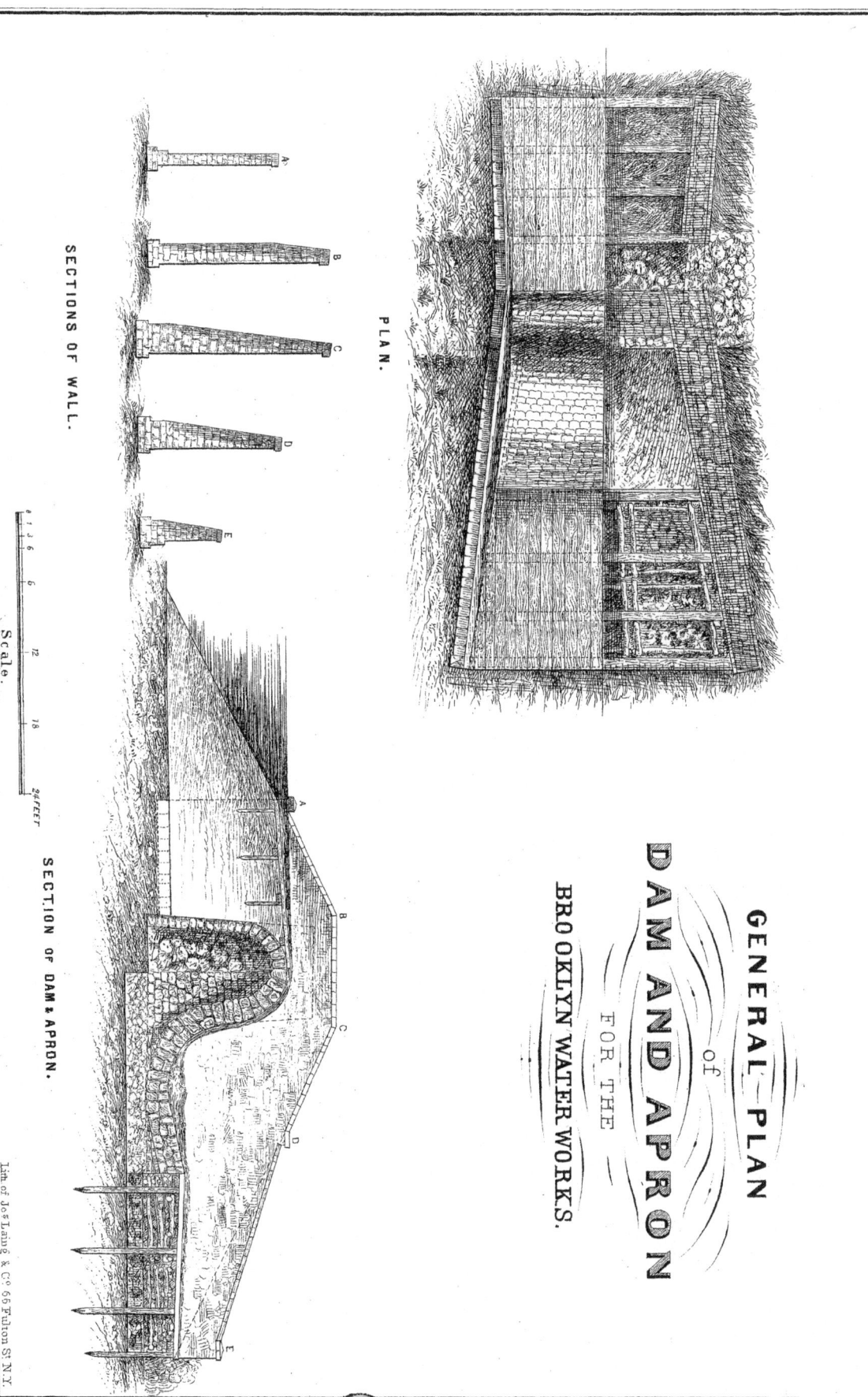

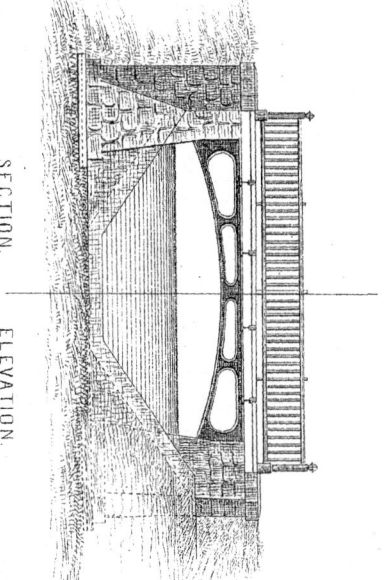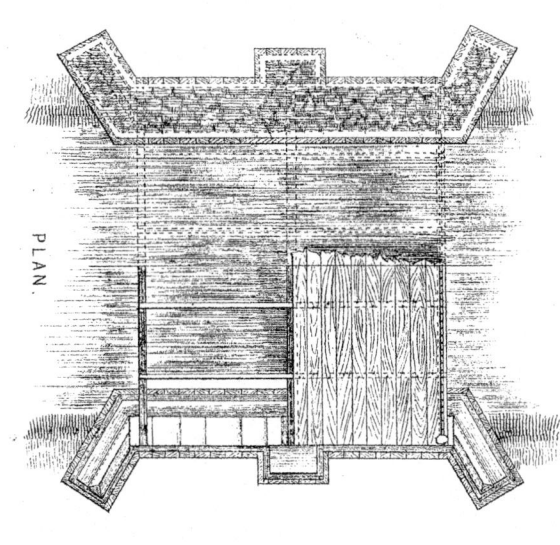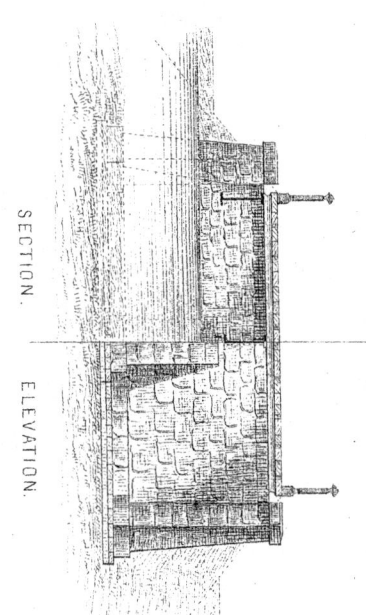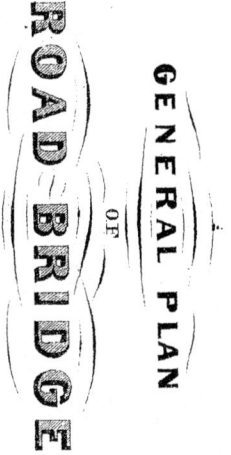

GENERAL PLAN
FOR
FARM BRIDGE.
BROOKLYN WATERWORKS.

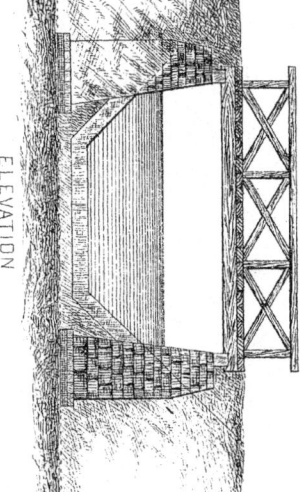

ELEVATION

ABUTMENT

PLAN

Scale of Feet

Plate Nº 21.

GENERAL PLAN FOR CREEK CULVERT
BROOKLYN WATER WORKS.

PLAN

END ELEVATION

CROSS SECTION

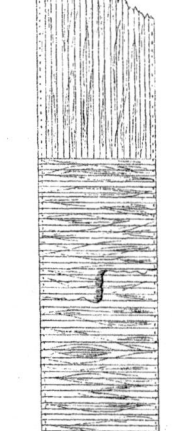

SECTION OF AQUEDUCT AND CULVERT

Lith. of Jos. Laing & Co. 65 Fulton St. N.Y.

Plate Nº 22

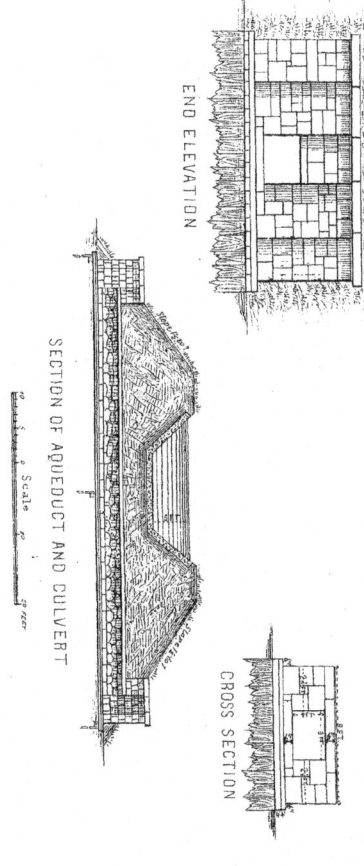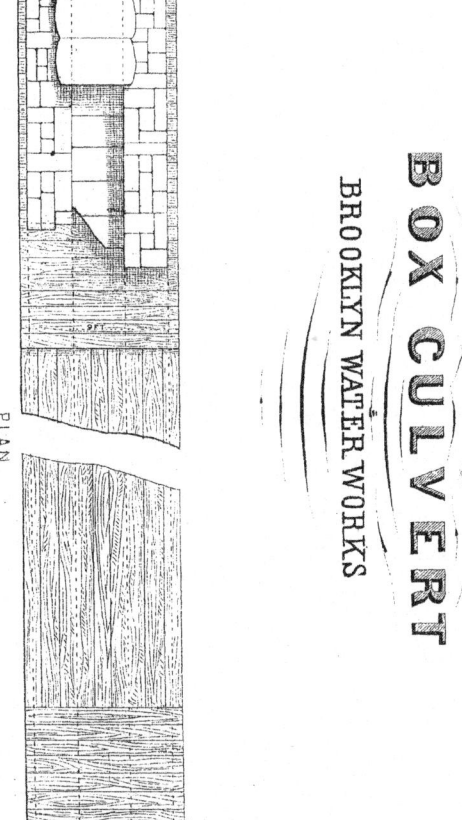

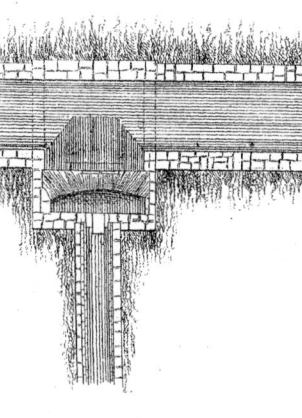

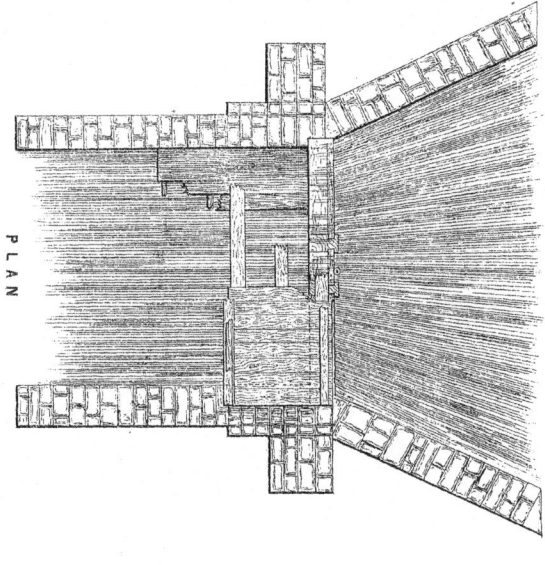

Plate Nº 26.

CROSS SECTIONS OF CONDUIT & CANAL BROOKLYN WATER WORKS.

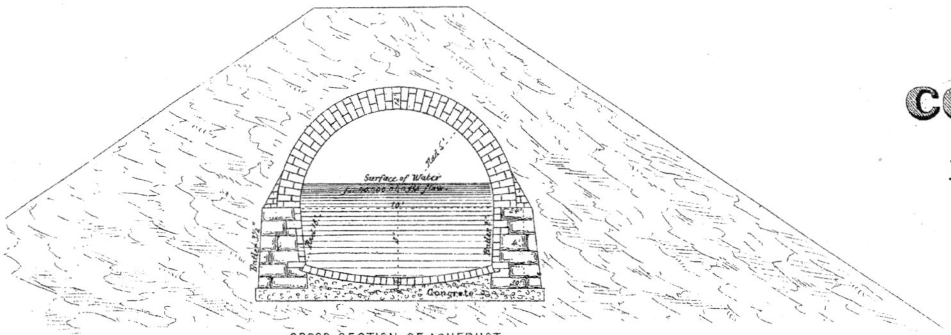

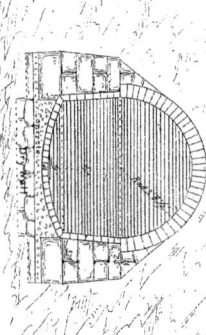

CROSS SECTION OF AQUEDUCT
BROOKLYN WATER WORKS

CROSS SECTION OF CROTON AQUEDUCT

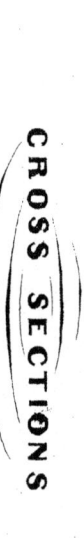

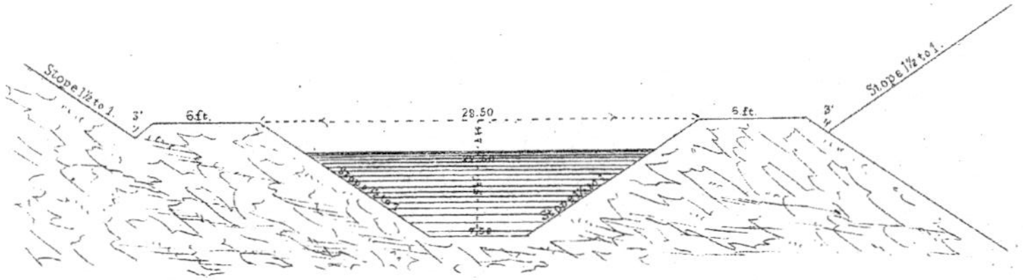

CROSS SECTION OF CANAL
EAST OF BAISELEYS.

Lith of Joˢ Laing & Cº 66 Fulton St. N.Y.

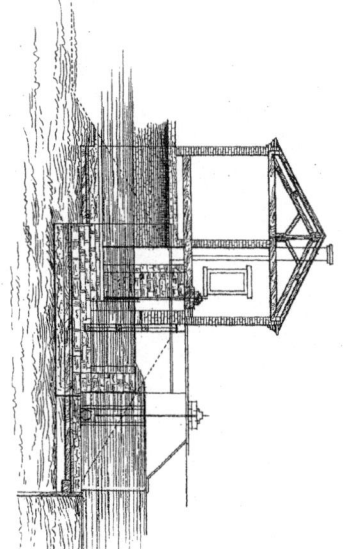

GENERAL PLAN
OF
APRON, GATE & KEEPER'S HOUSE
FOR THE
BROOKLYN WATER WORKS.

PLAN.

ELEVATION.

SECTION OF WASTE WEIR.

Plate Nº 27.

Lith. of Jos Laing & Co 66 Fulton St N.Y.

Printed in Dunstable, United Kingdom